**The Amazing Story
of Eric Davidson,
Survivor of the 1917
Halifax Explosion**

# The Blind Mechanic

NIMBUS
PUBLISHING
— NIMBUS.CA —

Foreword by Janet Kitz

**Marilyn Davidson Elliott**

Nimbus Publishing Limited
3660 Strawberry Hill Street, Halifax, NS, B3K 5A9
(902) 455-4286 nimbus.ca

NB1344

Cover photo: Eric Davidson working on a truck at Patterson Motors in Ottawa in 1950, using a feeler gauge to complete a valve job. (Davidson family photo)

Cover and interior design: Graphic Detail Inc.

Library and Archives Canada Cataloguing in Publication

Elliott, Marilyn Davidson, 1955-, author
The blind mechanic : the amazing story of Eric Davidson, survivor of the
1917 Halifax Explosion / Marilyn Davidson Elliott ; foreword by Janet Kitz.

Issued in print and electronic formats.
ISBN 978-1-77108-676-9 (softcover).—ISBN 978-1-77108-677-6 (HTML)

1. Davidson, Eric, 1915-2009. 2. Blind automobile mechanics—Nova
Scotia—Halifax—Biography. 3. Halifax Explosion, Halifax, N.S., 1917.
4. Biographies. I. Kitz, Janet F., 1930-, writer of foreword II. Title.

TL140.D39D39 2018    629.28'7092    C2018-902928-5
C2018-902929-3

Nimbus Publishing acknowledges the financial support for its publishing activities from the Government of Canada, the Canada Council for the Arts, and from the Province of Nova Scotia. We are pleased to work in partnership with the Province of Nova Scotia to develop and promote our creative industries for the benefit of all Nova Scotians.

*To Mom and Dad whose loving presence I felt with me
as I was writing.*

*To my children, Andrea and Matthew, and to my darling
granddaughters Ava, Isla, and Mary. It is for you that
I have written this book.*

*To John for your patience and understanding throughout.*

# Contents

Foreword    6

Preface    8

The Halifax Explosion    14

And Then It Happened    27

Recovery and Transition    36

School Days    50

Defying the Odds    60

A Love Match    69

One of the Boys    77

Raising a Family    83

Vacations    96

Shopping with Dad    101

Family Life    108

Grandma Georgina    119

Peepers and Croakers    132

A Passion for Antique Autos    145

The Golden Years    158

The Halifax Relief Commission Pension Fund    173

Commemorating the Halifax Explosion    181

Epilogue    191

Acknowledgements    195

Bibliography    197

# Foreword

Eric Davidson was introduced to me by his older sister, Marjorie, who attended many of the events held for survivors of the Halifax Explosion. There was obviously great affection between the two of them. Already knowing the cause of Eric's blindness, I was immediately impressed by the way he coped with it. There was no sign of self-pity or even blame for its cause.

At later social occasions, like tea parties, Eric was usually there, and managed without too much difficulty. He carried himself with his head slightly to one side, as if he were listening intently. Sound and touch were important for him.

One day he and I went walking in Point Pleasant Park. To my astonishment, he could identify fairly precisely where we were at any point. "The Quarry Pond must be there," he said. A little further on, he pointed to the other side, "The Martello Tower will be just up that little road."

The Halifax Relief Commission had been formed to restore the area affected by the Explosion and to disburse relief funds in the best possible manner. These funds had to cover pensions as long as any pensioner remained alive. The commission donated $100,000 for the building of the North End Library on Gottingen Street, a memorial to those lost in the Explosion.

Eric, in common with many other survivors, did not approve of this type of expenditure. "The money was meant to help the people who had suffered," he said, "not to put up buildings." Some money had already been spent on sidewalk improvements in the Hydrostone area. Money was being spent, but, despite increases in the cost of living, for a long time pensions did not quite keep up. Eric and I had many interesting discussions.

The chime of bells in the United Memorial Church, to which the Davidson family belonged, had been donated by another Explosion survivor. Eric did manage to pull the heavy levers and play the bells a few times. They are now in the tower on Fort Needham in the Explosion Monument, paid for by private donations not Relief Commission funds. Eric approved of that.

There are many stories about Eric and his mechanical abilities, especially with antique cars. He used to work on his own car in the garage attached to his house. Other enthusiasts often visited. On one occasion friends of mine were there. "Could we have the light on, Eric?" Basil asked.

"If you like," replied Eric. It made no difference to him.

Eric went to the School for the Blind. He told me that boys and girls were forbidden to socialize, as it was believed that blindness could be passed on to future generations.

"My blindness was certainly not hereditary," Eric said.

—Janet Kitz, author of *Shattered City; Survivors: Children of the Halifax Explosion*

# Preface

When I was just a little girl, I realized that my father was a special person. Not only because he was my father and I adored him, but because whenever we were out in public people gravitated to him. He was like a magnet. People wanted to shake my father's hand and speak with him and they were always smiling and happy to be around him. It became routine. In time, I came to know that my father was not just special—he was extraordinary.

My father, Eric Davidson, was a survivor of the Halifax Explosion. As a toddler he was blinded when the munitions ship *Mont Blanc* exploded in Halifax Harbour on December 6, 1917.

From childhood, my father dreamed of becoming an automobile mechanic. He was denied the opportunity to formally train at a trade school because he was blind. Not willing to accept this rejection as defeat, he schooled himself and worked for years honing his skills to become a qualified auto mechanic. His determination was rewarded. Dad had a successful career as an accomplished auto mechanic for the City of Halifax for twenty-five years.

How Dad chose to live his life and how he overcame the challenges of living in absolute darkness for ninety-two years is nothing short of remarkable. He embraced life and faced each day with a positive attitude, fortitude, and most assuredly with grace and humour. By approaching life as he did, Dad lived a very full and rewarding life.

My father was not willing to be a victim of the Halifax Explosion. He did not consider himself disabled and the word "disabled" was never used in our home to describe our father. Dad was ambitious and fiercely independent although he said he was just plain stubborn. Most of all, Dad just wanted to be an ordinary man and enjoy all the wonders that life had to offer.

A steadfast North Ender all of his life, Eric Davidson was an iconic figure, being one of the most recognized survivors of the Halifax Explosion as he walked the city streets with his white cane. Local people who did not know him personally knew him as the man who was blinded in the Explosion or as the *blind mechanic*.

Dad was never bitter about his handicap. The fact that he was blinded was of small consequence to him for he believed his family was lucky to survive the Halifax Explosion. When he was interviewed for the A&E television program *Sea Tales* in 1992 he said, "We were all injured and we all recovered and we were one of the luckiest families in the city, I think."

My father did not seek recognition; it found him. It was most unusual for someone without sight to have a career as an auto mechanic and to accomplish all the things that my father did in his lifetime. The media, like everyone who met Dad, were fascinated by him for he was truly a phenomenon. They recognized that his story of survival and accomplishment was one of great public interest.

Consequently, throughout his lifetime the media featured many stories about him on film, television, radio, and in magazines and newspapers. In 1975, the National Film Board of Canada produced a documentary about him, *Just One of the Boys.*

My father had a tremendous impact on my life and I have always wanted to write a book about him. However, I knew that Dad was extremely humble and he would have considered a book about him to be boastful. So I did not do any more than think about writing while he was living. Following his death in 2009, I began to contemplate this project although I was apprehensive that I could actually undertake such a huge endeavour and do it justice. In conversation with a friend who is an accomplished author, she gave me the push I needed to settle down and begin my research and writing. It was the proverbial boot in the backside. The time had come to tell the world about this wonderful man I was blessed to call Dad.

Considering to write a book and then to actually write it are two different matters. I wanted to honour my father's memory and accurately tell his life story but I had never written a book before. Where to start? A stroke of good fortune for me was that my mother had meticulously saved personal letters, documents, and photographs over the years. Mom saved virtually everything, and I am most grateful to her for that. I also have the luxury of video footage of my father from various media sources, along with scores of newspaper and magazine articles written about him. With my personal memories of my father, these documents, letters, photos, and media productions gave me an excellent resource to draw upon as I wrote.

Some of my resources are also now my most cherished possessions. I am referring to my father's audio recordings. He carried his tape recorder with him like people nowadays carry their cellphones. It was ever present during his leisure time. He recorded my brothers and me singing and playing when we were children, he recorded nature sounds such as spring peepers and frogs, he recorded locomotives and the engines of various antique cars that he owned, and he even recorded himself playing the banjo.

I find it emotional to listen to my father's gentle voice tenderly coaxing me to come sit by him when I was a two-year-old. I feel Dad beside me as I listen to his voice and I have chuckled plenty and shed more than a few tears throughout this process.

I am fortunate that Dad captured so many of our family's precious moments together and that the recordings survived. Some recordings are now sixty years old. I have had some of them transferred to CD format so that my family will share these recordings for generations to come. Dad could not have known what a cherished gift these recordings are for my brothers and me.

Finally, I gathered information from records held at the Nova Scotia Archives and from Veterans Affairs Canada. With these resources, personal

Eric (two) and his sister Marjorie (four) pictured in Halifax in 1917 before the Explosion. Eric is looking coyly at the camera.

materials, and with my own memories and the memories and stories of family and friends, I have put together what I believe is a true representation of my father's life.

The last television interview my father gave was with well-known local television personality Liz Rigney in February 2008 when he was living in Berwick, Nova Scotia. Liz recently shared her memories of that interview with me: "He taught me so much by just embracing what he could do, not avoiding the things he couldn't do. It was as though he just said, 'Okay, I want to do this, so how do I do that?' never wondering IF he could, more so HOW it would be accomplished. That's a powerful lesson."

There are so many heart-wrenching and truly sad family stories that have come from the disaster of the Halifax Explosion. Families who lost so many loved ones that day, fathers who watched helplessly as their family burned inside their wrecked homes, children who one minute had loving parents and the next minute were orphaned. My father's story of survival is a positive and uplifting story with a happy ending. I want to share his story with the world, and if only one reader is inspired to work harder to reach their goal or to take a more positive approach in their daily life, then I will have done my father proud.

June 16, 1919
Dr. G. B. Cutten
Rehabilitation Dept.
Halifax Relief Commission
City

Dear Sir,

I wonder if I may ask you if it would be possible to secure an old motor car of any kind that is ready for the junk pile for our little boy Eric to play with. As perhaps you know he is extremely fond of motor cars and I thought it might be possible to get an old car that was of no use to anyone and put it in the yard for him to amuse himself with this summer. Last summer when living on the south common I was in the habit of taking him to the Wanderers Grounds when there were any games on and as there were several old cars stored there since the Explosion that did not seem to belong to anybody he would play with the old cars for hours and they were a great source of enjoyment for him. Could not one of these cars be secured? I do not know whom to apply to so thought I would write you in the hope that you may be willing to assist us in this respect. We will greatly appreciate anything you may do for Eric in this matter.

I remain,
Yours sincerely,
John W. Davidson

# The Halifax Explosion

Halifax was a robust city in 1917 with a population of roughly fifty thousand. It was thriving industrially and becoming a cultural centre complete with theatres, restaurants, libraries, and more. Government offices and banking institutions were located in the South End along with the more affluent of Halifax society, while industries and the working-class citizens of Halifax were mostly situated in the North End community of Richmond. The name Richmond was given to the area north of the Wellington barracks (now CFB Stadacona) and east of Gottingen Street in the mid-1800s when goods were brought from Richmond, Virginia, and landed at wharves located near the present shipyards.

Originally, Richmond had been a farming village, but by the late 1850s a railway skirted the shoreline and Richmond eventually became industrialized with factories such as the Nova Scotia Sugar Refinery, the Richmond Printing Company, Hillis & Sons Foundry, and the Nova Scotia Cotton Manufacturing Company to name a few. In 1877, the Intercolonial Railway opened the North Street Station at the foot of North Street.

Industry workers settled on the Richmond slope, a steep hill that rises up from the harbour. At the top of the hill more than one hundred and twenty metres above the harbour is Fort Needham, which was at one time a strategic naval installation constructed upon a drumlin. The dictionary definition of a drumlin is a glacial formation, an elongated hill that is shaped like an inverted spoon or a half-buried egg. Fort Needham was active during the American and French Revolutions but after the War of 1812, the fort was decommissioned and was left to deteriorate to the point that by 1917 there was little evidence of its existence.

Richmond residents were mostly of Scottish and Irish heritage and the predominant religions were Roman Catholic, Anglican, Presbyterian, or Methodist. Four churches served the Richmond community: St. Joseph's Roman Catholic, St. Mark's Anglican, Grove Presbyterian, and Kaye Street Methodist. Churches were the nerve centres of Halifax-area communities in the early 1900s and as such Richmond churches played a major role in the everyday life of the community. Religious and social events and community gatherings took place there.

Streets ran up the Richmond slope from Campbell Road to Fort Needham and Gottingen Street with side streets running north to south crossing at right angles. By 1917, these streets were dotted with hundreds of wooden-framed houses stretching along the shoreline of Campbell Road all the way up the hilly slope to Gottingen Street. The source of heating for these homes was coal or wood. Wharves and warehouses lined the Richmond waterfront and trains ran along the harbour and the shores of the Bedford Basin to points beyond delivering goods and passengers to and fro daily. It was a bustling little community.

Halifax was an important city in wartime and it was a beehive of activity in 1917. The First World War was in its third year and convoys formed up in Bedford Basin just a short distance north of Richmond. Bedford Basin is an oval-shaped sheltered body of deep water that lies at the northern end of Halifax Harbour. The harbour itself is approximately four miles long and the basin, like Halifax Harbour, remains open and free of ice all year round. The basin was an ideal place to assemble convoys that would be heading overseas with troops, much-needed supplies, and munitions for the war effort.

Thursday, December 6, 1917, dawned a pleasant, sunny, and surprisingly warm day. Richmond households buzzed with the usual morning preparations. Men were heading off to work and children were readying themselves for school. The Protestant children went to Richmond School on

Roome Street and the Roman Catholic children went to St. Joseph's School on Kaye Street. The majority of Richmond men were labourers employed at the nearby HMC dockyards, the North Street Station, and the Canadian Government Railways, the Acadia Sugar Refinery, and Hillis & Sons Foundry. As was customary at this time, Richmond women stayed at home caring for their children and managing the home.

While Richmond residents were busy with their morning routines, something was happening right below them in the harbour. Two ships were on a collision course in The Narrows, a location where the harbour narrows to join Bedford Basin. The *Imo*, a Norwegian steamer, had just left the safety of Bedford Basin and was heading south in the harbour. Painted on its side were the words Belgian Relief to protect it from German submarines. The *Imo* was a long and narrow steamship at 131.3 metres long and 13.8 metres wide, carrying a crew of thirty-nine men commanded by Captain Haakon From.

The *Mont Blanc*, a French munitions freighter commanded by Captain Aimé Le Médec, was heading north toward Bedford Basin to join a convoy of supply ships that would be leaving Halifax soon to cross the Atlantic for England. The *Mont Blanc*, smaller than the *Imo*, measured 97.5 metres in length and 13.7 metres wide. She was carrying a lethal cargo of 2,300 tons of picric acid, 200 tons of TNT, 10 tons of gun cotton, and on the deck 35 tons of benzol in large metal barrels. This combination of highly explosive materials made the *Mont Blanc* a floating bomb.

Both ships had Halifax Harbour pilots on-board. Piloting the *Imo* that morning was Pilot William Hayes and piloting the *Mont Blanc* was Pilot Francis Mackey.

The *Imo* was off course and steaming quickly toward the slow-moving *Mont Blanc*. There were signal blasts from ship to ship; however, the *Imo* maintained its course, bearing down on the *Mont Blanc*. The *Mont Blanc* and the *Imo* both took last-minute manoeuvres in an effort to avoid a collision. However, it was too little too late and at approximately 8:45 A.M., the *Imo* cut into the starboard bow of the *Mont Blanc*.

The *Imo* reversed its engines to pull away from the *Mont Blanc*, creating sparks, which ignited the picric acid and set fire to the drums of benzol on the deck of the *Mont Blanc*. The fire spread rapidly while the crew tried unsuccessfully to scuttle the ship. As the *Mont Blanc* floated toward the Richmond piers, witnesses observed two boats lowered from the *Mont Blanc* as its crew and the harbour pilot abandoned the burning ship and rowed hastily to the Dartmouth shore. The abandoned *Mont Blanc* continued to float in the direction of the Richmond piers.

A huge fireball lit up the morning sky as *Mont Blanc* burned. Hundreds of people converged to the dockside. Men on their way to work and children on their way to school stopped to watch the inferno. Richmond residents in the assumed safety of their homes stood at their windows watching. Dartmouth residents in Tufts Cove and the Mi'kmaw settlement of Turtle Grove watched the spectacle in the harbour just as their Richmond counterparts did.

The West Street station of the Halifax Fire Department responded to the call of a fire on-board a boat near Pier 6. When they arrived at Pier 6 with their brand new fire truck, Patricia, the crew of the tugboat *Stella Maris* was valiantly attempting to tow the burning ship away from the Richmond piers. Their efforts were in vain.

At approximately 9:04 A.M., roughly twenty minutes after the collision, *Mont Blanc* exploded near Pier 6 in Richmond. The ship was blown apart. A huge mushroom-shaped cloud formed over the harbour. A shock wave radiated away from the explosion and was felt in Truro, some sixty miles away. The blast created a massive tidal wave, which washed up over Campbell Road in Richmond and Turtle Grove in Dartmouth, sucking injured and lifeless victims with it as the wave receded. Many bodies were never recovered. Never before had such an explosion been detonated in the midst of thousands of people. The Halifax Explosion was the most powerful non-nuclear explosion in the world. To this day, it remains the worst disaster in Canadian history.

The cities of Halifax and Dartmouth were both rocked. Richmond suffered a direct hit and in an instant was obliterated from the face of the earth. The blast from the Explosion killed nearly two thousand people; most died instantly. Approximately nine thousand people were injured, twenty-five thousand were left homeless, and over two hundred children became

Smoke cloud from the Explosion is shown in this photo, one of few taken moments after the disaster.

orphans. The Mi'kmaw settlement at Turtle Grove was destroyed, leaving nine dead and many injured.

On the western side of the Richmond slopes nestled into the southern shore of the Bedford Basin was Africville, an African Nova Scotian community. While Africville was protected from the direct blast of the Explosion, homes were badly damaged and there were four known casualties from that community.

There were casualties on-board boats and ships docked and operating near Pier 6 as well. The SS *Curaca* lost thirty-two men, five of them from the tiny Scottish island of Barra. The *Stella Maris, Calonne,* HMS *Highflyer,* the *Picton,* and several more ships lost crew. The *Imo* lost seven crew, including Captain From and Pilot Hayes, while one member of the crew of the *Mont Blanc* died from injuries he sustained while attempting to escape the blast.

The scene in Richmond that day was one of absolute devastation. Hundreds of corpses littered the ground, hideously destroyed bodies strewn about, some missing limbs and some bodies missing heads. Homes and

Rescuers are shown searching for survivors in the devastated Richmond neighbourhood where most of the casualties occurred. The Davidson family home was one of many destroyed in the Explosion.

businesses were flattened, trees were uprooted, and the area looked as though a tornado had swept through. Not a house remained standing in Richmond as fires from overturned stoves burned amidst the collapsed houses. A black rain fell from the sky, covering everything and everybody with an oily residue. The four Richmond churches and the schools were destroyed.

Survivors covered in the black oily residue wandered about bewildered and in shock. Many had their clothing ripped from their bodies by the explosion's backdraft. Others suffered grotesque injuries such as facial lacerations, vicious open wounds, broken and lacerated limbs, and partially detached limbs. The sights were ghastly. Many survivors thought they had been attacked by the Germans. Hundreds of survivors died, as they lay trapped in burning houses or from exposure waiting to be rescued from the wreckage of their homes. Because coal was stored in the basements of houses, fires continued to burn in Richmond for days following the explosion. A soldier recently returned from the war is reported to have said that Richmond looked worse than the war-ravaged battlefields he had seen overseas.

Roome Street School was one of the many buildings destroyed in the Explosion.

Archibald MacMechan, who was later appointed by the executive committee of the Halifax Relief Commission to record an official history of the Halifax Explosion, wrote in his report *The Halifax Disaster*:

> Under the wreckage of Richmond that morning there were hundreds of human beings injured, but in some cases unhurt, who were to die by fire. The mind refuses to dwell upon the horrors of that morning men and women like ourselves, broken, bruised, bleeding, half-conscious or worse still, uninjured but imprisoned in the wreckage and the inexorable flames coming swiftly nearer. The pity of it…to see your own perish in torment before your eyes and being impotent to help. All that morning a tall silvery column of smoke rose to the sky above the burning North End…the streets were filled with the strangest apparitions: men, women and children with their faces streaming with blood from wounds dealt by the flying glass, faces chalk-white with terror and streaked with red, faces black with the "black rain" and smeared with blood. The dead, the dying and the severely injured lay about the streets, amid ghastly fragments of

what had been human beings' heads and limbs….Some were dazed and semi-conscious from the shock. Some were uttering shrieks of pain and terror. Some were helping injured people away or trying to extricate them from the ruin of their houses. There was no order or direction.[1]

Dr. Willis Bryant Moore was travelling on a relief train from Kentville to Halifax on December 6, 1917, only a few hours after the *Mont Blanc* exploded. In his personal narrative to the Halifax Disaster Record Office, Dr. Moore's eyewitness account vividly describes the totality of Richmond's destruction and brings the reader to that moment in time such that they feel they are riding the train with him.

Approaching Richmond the completeness of destruction was increasingly apparent, and when we finally left our train to walk until we met faster means to approach our destination, the City Hall where we were directed to report for distribution, no word except appalling would indicate the horrors of the scene. To the writer it seemed like an actual realization of the scene picture of Dante's Inferno, which he had witnessed at the moving picture theatre some years ago. The peculiar blackness of the whole devastated area lightened by lurid jets of flame springing from the crater-like cellars of the ruins, with the fantastic shapes of those around the destroyed homes, searching and probing vainly for their lost ones, and springing back from the shooting flames like imps of Hades, and the blackened tree trunks in the region standing gaunt and spectral like, as it were, the outpost sentinels of their kingdom, with the rows of blackened and often half naked and twisted bodies of the dead, through which we picked our way, made a weird and desolate spectacle, the depressing effects of which could only be understood by those unfortunate enough to witness it.[2]

Unfortunately, there was no warning for the hundreds of onlookers who gathered along Campbell Road and near the piers to watch the ship

1 G. Metson, *The Halifax Explosion*: December 6, 1917. (Toronto: McGraw Hill Ryerson, 1978.) p. 18.
2 Metson, p. 107–108.

burning in the harbour. Nor was there any warning for the thousands who innocently stood by their windows watching the fire or for those who were going about their business in Richmond on that December morning, possibly oblivious to what was happening. Because so many residents in North End Halifax and Dartmouth were standing at their windows watching the *Mont Blanc,* there were a massive number of eye injuries from shattered windows.

No family in Richmond was left untouched. Husbands rushed home to find wives and children dead and their homes on fire or destroyed. Children who survived ran to their homes only to find them either flattened or in flames and that one or both parents, as well as siblings, had perished. Children who had been part of a family were suddenly alone and orphaned. So many tragic souls. Many families suffered a tremendous loss of life with multiple casualties. In addition, there were the injured survivors, many of them children now orphaned or disabled in one way or another.

The first to offer assistance and to rescue survivors were neighbours who were uninjured. They pulled survivors from burning homes, bandaged wounds, and helped transport the injured to hospital mostly by horse-and-buggy, as there were very few automobiles in working-class Richmond in 1917. Halifax-area firefighters and police responded immediately for rescue and recovery operations. Residents outside the area of devastation rushed to Richmond to assist in rescue operations. Residents of Halifax neighbourhoods where homes were undamaged opened their homes and offered food, clothing, and shelter to the thousands of people left homeless. Towns and communities across Nova Scotia responded as well with food, clothing, medical supplies, and shelter for refugees.

As Halifax was a military city, the response from the military was immediate. They organized rescue and recovery operations, set up temporary hospitals, and provided medical assistance for the injured. Military vehicles transported the injured to hospitals and the dead to morgues. Private vehicles were commandeered for the same purpose. A perimeter was set up around the disaster zone and the military organized patrols to prevent looting.

Rescue efforts were hampered when a dreadful blizzard hit Halifax on December 7, 1917, the day following the Explosion. Countless people who

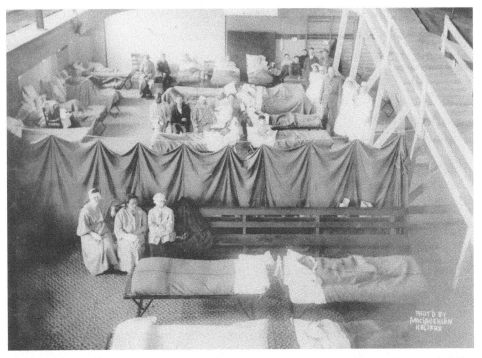

An emergency hospital set up at the YMCA to treat the wounded and suffering. The scene depicted here was similar to one at the Halifax Ladies' College where Eric was taken.

had survived died of exposure as they lay trapped in the rubble of their homes and buried under the snow waiting for rescue.

Halifax-area doctors and nurses worked without rest for forty-eight hours treating a multitude of hideous injuries. The medical professionals accustomed to routine minor ailments found themselves overwhelmed with thousands of injuries similar to those that would be sustained on a battlefield. There were not enough beds, so hundreds of injured survivors were laid out on hospital floors awaiting treatment. Injuries were triaged with the most urgent treated first.

Within hours of the disaster, doctors, nurses, and much-needed medical supplies arrived on relief trains from neighbouring towns such as Truro, Kentville, Amherst, and New Glasgow. These rural doctors and nurses worked around the clock with the Halifax-area medical professionals treating the injured and dying as they arrived at hospitals. Dr. W. B. Moore who was assigned to Camp Hill Hospital wrote:

> Many of us had seen terrible sights of human tragedies and suffering but nothing like this in the immensity of the number and the frightful and varied character of the injuries. Men, women and children of all sorts and classes were literally packed in the wards like sardines in a box, the cots all occupied and the floors covered so that it was often difficult to step between them.[3]

On December 8, 1917, two days after the Explosion, a train from Boston, Massachusetts, arrived with medical personnel and essential medical supplies. A lot of gratitude has rightly been given to Boston for the medical and financial aid it generously delivered to Halifax. However, for the first forty-eight hours following the Explosion, local and rural Nova Scotia doctors and nurses worked in the most cramped of conditions and under immense strain before the Massachusetts relief arrived. Unfortunately, the massive contribution of the local medical profession has been much overlooked in the years following the Halifax Explosion. Yet, they were instrumental in relieving the suffering of thousands in those first two critical days.

As news of the disaster spread, financial aid began pouring in from all over Canada, the United States, and around the world. The Halifax Relief Commission was established by the Government of Canada in January 1918 to assist victims. The commission was funded by $27 million of public and private contributions and empowered to provide emergency housing and relief to victims of the Halifax Explosion, to recover the dead, and to clear, rebuild, and repair the North End of Halifax.

The people of Halifax were incensed and wanted to know who was to blame for this great disaster. How did two ships collide in Halifax Harbour with each ship carrying an experienced harbour pilot on-board? A legal inquiry was held in Halifax in an attempt to determine the cause of the collision and to lay blame at the feet of those responsible. The inquiry determined that Captain Le Médec of the *Mont Blanc* and Pilot Francis

3  Metson, p. 109.

Mackey were responsible. That decision was eventually appealed to the Privy Council in London, England, which concluded that both the *Imo* and the *Mont Blanc* captains and harbour pilots were equally responsible.

As is so often the case in dire situations, there were many who did their best to avert the disaster. Nineteen of the *Stella Maris* crew were killed as they tried to tow the *Mont Blanc* away from Pier 6. These brave men sacrificed their lives to save the lives of others.

The Halifax Fire Department suffered the greatest loss of firefighter lives in Canadian history that day. Nine firefighters, including Chief Edward Condon, died responding to the fire aboard the *Mont Blanc*.

Vince Coleman, a train dispatcher for the Canadian Government Railways working at the depot station near Pier 6 in Richmond, received word that the *Mont Blanc* was carrying explosives. He remained on duty sending Morse code messages warning incoming passenger trains not to enter Halifax as a ship was on fire in the harbour and would explode. He died, but his heroic action saved lives.

Could anyone who survived the horrors of the Halifax Explosion ever fully recover from the trauma? Doctors, nurses, and those involved with rescue operations witnessed gory and gruesome sights that would remain imprinted in their memories forever. Many struggled with the reality of what they witnessed and found it difficult to live with the horrors they were exposed to following the Explosion.

Survivors bore mental as well as physical injuries for the remainder of their lives. Possibly the most heartbreaking cases were parents unable to rescue their children who lay trapped in the burning rubble of their home. There is no actual recorded number of suicides following the Explosion but it is known that there were those who could not cope. Some survivors turned to alcohol to wash away their nightmarish memories. This only served to exacerbate their suffering. Others tried to escape the memory of the Explosion and the loss of loved ones by moving to other parts of Canada, the New England states, or elsewhere, hoping for a new start. Doubtful they escaped the trauma of their memories.

The majority of Richmond survivors chose to remain in Halifax though. They were resilient enough to return to Richmond to rebuild their community. Within a few years, survivors had rebuilt Richmond School and St. Joseph's School as well as St. Joseph's Church and St. Mark's Church. The congregations of Grove Presbyterian and Kaye Street Methodist banded together and built United Memorial Church on Kaye Street. While their churches were being rebuilt, the congregations held their weekly services in and shared use of a temporary church that was called the Tar Paper Church.

For some years, the Explosion-ravaged streets on the Richmond slopes facing the harbour lay empty, as there was little interest in rebuilding there so soon after the Explosion. Much of the reconstruction was west of Gottingen Street in and around the area now known as the Hydrostone.

The Hydrostone neighbourhood was designed by architect Thomas Adams to provide housing for working-class families displaced by the Explosion. The district is an English-garden suburb design of row houses in groups of four or six with a large two-storey house at the east end of each street and a tree-lined boulevard on every street but one. The houses are constructed of concrete block and fireproof materials. The Hydrostone Market on Young Street offers a variety of unique shops, restaurants, and services and is a major tourist attraction. The Hydrostone was and still is one of the better-designed residential areas of the city and is now designated a National Historic Site of Canada.

The Halifax Explosion was designated as a national historic event in 2016 as the disaster had profound consequences locally and nationally.

Today, there are many descendants of Halifax Explosion victims living in this neighbourhood. The name Richmond is no longer used to identify the community. Instead, people refer to it as the Hydrostone district. Regardless of the name, this area of North End Halifax is a strong, diverse, and vibrant community risen from the ashes of the Halifax Explosion.

# And Then It Happened

Like many Nova Scotians, my family arrived from Scotland as immigrants. Our Davidson ancestry goes back several hundred years to the quaint hamlet of Boarhills near Kingsbarns in the East Neuk of Fife, Scotland. Boarhills and Kingsbarns lie along the scenic east coast of Scotland and are approximately five miles from historic St. Andrews.

The Davidsons worked as farmhands on an estate in Kingsbarns while living in neighbouring Boarhills. Coming forward a few centuries, my great-great-grandfather James Davidson, born in 1831 to William Davidson and Mary Swan, left Boarhills to work in Glasgow as a joiner or carpenter. He married Jane McNaughton from nearby Alva, and in 1853 their son William was born in Glasgow, Scotland. However, something tragic happened to James and Jane shortly after William was born. There is no record of what happened to William's parents but it is possible that they fell victim to cholera, which was ravaging Glasgow in the early 1850s. William was raised by his grandparents William and Mary Davidson in Boarhills.

William, like his father before him, left Fife and made his way to Glasgow where he found work as a locomotive engineer. In 1874, he married Jeannie McFadyen of Kilmarnock. Shortly after their first child, James, was born, William and Jeannie moved to Newcastle upon Tyne in northeast

England. William was employed with the railway there as well. Two more
children were born in Newcastle upon Tyne, Rachel in 1880 and John
William in 1882. John was my grandfather.

In the early 1880s, the Canadian railway was blossoming and advertising
in the UK in an effort to recruit men to work in Canada. William foresaw a
better life in Canada for his family so he bought passage on the Allen Line
ocean steamship *Manitoban* that departed from Glasgow on May 5, 1883,
and arrived in Quebec City on May 18, 1883.

The family of five made their way from Quebec to Halifax where William
had secured a job as a locomotive engineer with the Intercolonial Railway.
William settled his family in the North End working-class community of
Richmond in 1883. Eight years later in 1891, a fourth child, Victor, was
born to William and Jeannie in Halifax. Near the turn of the century,
William moved his family to South Forks, Cape Breton, where they lived for
roughly ten years while William was employed with the railway.

John returned to Halifax from Cape Breton to seek employment and by
1911 he was twenty-nine years old and working as a chief clerk in the Stores
Department at the HMC Halifax Dockyards. John was a handsome man
of medium height and build with lovely, curly auburn-coloured hair. While
he had a calm and gentle disposition and he was soft-spoken, he could be
tenacious. He was a very religious man and, being quite musical, he was
a member of the choir at Grove Presbyterian Church on Duffus Street in
Richmond.

It was at church that John met Georgina Williams. Georgina was
attractive, tall for a woman, roughly five foot eight, with a slim build, dark
hair, and a very confident personality. Georgina's people, the Williamses,
were tall and sturdy-framed people who were also of Scottish descent. Her
family had originally lived in the rural farming community of Ellershouse
about thirty-five miles outside of Halifax but had recently relocated to
Richmond.

John and Georgina were married in Grove Presbyterian Church in 1912.
They rented a small home at 81 Roome Street in Richmond where their first
child, Marjorie, was born in late 1913. Less than two years later on May 10,
1915, my father, John Eric, was born. His parents always called him by his

Eric's paternal grandparents, Jeannie, seated at left, and William Davidson standing beside her.
Eric's father, John, standing at right. James, Rachel, and young Victor seated by his mother, 1901.

middle name, Eric. By 1917, the family had moved to 584 Gottingen Street, which was located at the southwest corner of Duffus and Gottingen Streets.

John had no Davidson relatives living in Halifax at this time. His brother James was married and living in Manitoba and his sister Rachel was married and living in Sydney, Nova Scotia. His younger brother, Victor, was a military doctor serving with the Canadian Expeditionary Force in France during the First World War, and his parents, William and Jeannie, were then living in Truro. Victor and his parents would subsequently settle in Saint John, New Brunswick, at the end of the war and Rachel and her family settled in New York.

Conversely, Georgina had many relatives living nearby in Richmond, mainly on Duffus, Acadia, and Rector Streets. She had three brothers and four sisters, all married with young families, so little Eric and his sister Marjorie had lots of cousins to play with and they spent a great deal of time with their Williams relatives.

The first two and one half years of Eric's life were typical of most children in Richmond at that time. He was a chubby little toddler, fair-haired and rosy cheeked with lovely blue eyes. Just like any little boy his age, he was inquisitive and active and he especially enjoyed playing outside with Marjorie. He and Marjorie were much loved by their parents and they would soon have another sibling to play with, as Georgina was expecting a baby in the spring of 1918. By all accounts, the young family was contented and living a normal Richmond family life. That was soon about to change.

In the early morning hours of December 6, 1917, Georgina had a dream in which she was told to gather her family and leave Halifax. This was a forerunner of tragedy for the family and Georgina was shaken. She felt it was real and she woke John and told him of the dream. He responded to her as most husbands would, stating that it was only a dream and that she should go back to sleep. Neither of them could have foreseen the horror that was about to unfold a few hours later.

And so it was on December 6, 1917, that John left for work while little Eric, Marjorie, and their mother stood looking toward the harbour watching while the *Mont Blanc* burned, lighting up the winter sky. Eric was running his toy train engine back and forth on the windowsill as he watched the fire.

Marjorie (two) and Eric (about six months old) sitting on their mother, Georgina's, lap in the autumn of 1915. Georgina never really recovered from the tragedy of her son's injury.

Marjorie stood nearby. Ships' horns were making a commotion down in the harbour, and Eric asked his mother why the horns were blowing.

Georgina placed two knives on the table and slid them along toward each other to demonstrate to the children how ships would pass by each other while travelling in opposite directions in the harbour. She explained to Marjorie and Eric that ships blasted their horns as they approached each other to send signals of intended direction and movement. Living in Halifax had well acquainted Georgina to the sound of ships signalling down in the harbour on a daily basis. The ships she spoke of were the French munitions ship *Mont Blanc* and the Belgian Relief ship *Imo* although Georgina did not know the names at that time. Georgina had no inkling of the danger that was only minutes away. And then it happened!

At approximately 9:04 A.M., the *Mont Blanc* blew up, and Georgina's nightmare became reality. In an instant, the house shook violently and collapsed in upon the family. The window that Eric had been looking through exploded inwards, sending shards of shattered glass into his face, viciously penetrating his beautiful blue eyes. In that moment, he was plunged into darkness for the rest of his life.

Georgina and Marjorie had moved away from the window before the explosion, and as a result their injuries were less severe. Marjorie was burned by scalding water when the stove overturned and Georgina had lacerations from flying glass to one arm and her neck and she was bleeding profusely. She too was burned by the water. They were all trapped inside the collapsed house. Georgina was rendered unconscious and, when she regained consciousness, Marjorie and Eric were screaming.

Georgina struggled to make her way to her children through the rubble. She managed to locate Marjorie and Eric and drew them in close to her body, trying vainly to console them and to protect them from further injury. When she looked at Eric's face, with glass penetrating his eyes, she went weak with despair. He was clawing at his eyes, and Georgina did her best to restrain him. It was all she could do to maintain her own sanity. At the same time Georgina's mind was racing. *What on earth just happened?* Georgina soon realized that her eerie dream from the night before had come to fruition. All she could do was try to comfort her children.

John was walking down Duffus Street toward the harbour on his way to work at the dockyard at the time of the Explosion. He could see smoke rising from a ship on fire down in the harbour near Pier 6. Adults and children were rushing past him down the hill to catch a closer glimpse of the fire. He thought he might take a closer look too. Then, without warning, he was thrown against a tree and he lost consciousness. He did not know how long he was unconscious, but when he came to he saw that his boots and some of his clothing had been torn off and all around him there was mayhem. People were running in all directions or wandering about like sleepwalkers, wringing their hands. Some people were lying in the streets not moving. The sights were ghastly. He could not fathom why he was witnessing such horrible sights and he wondered what on earth had happened. Was Halifax attacked by the

Germans? Fearing for his family, yet still unsteady, he stood up and began to make his way back up the hill to his home on Gottingen Street.

When he arrived home, John was shocked to find that the house had collapsed. Immediately his heart sank. He called to Georgina and he thought he heard her answer him. He also thought he could hear his children crying inside. But he wasn't certain, for there was so much commotion on the streets around him. John clawed and dug at the rubble like a madman to get to his family. It seemed like it took an eternity for him to reach them and when he did he was overjoyed to find Georgina and the children alive! But his joy quickly turned to anguish.

Georgina was bleeding profusely, little Marjorie was suffering from burns and crying, and, worst of all, his baby boy Eric had his face and eyes torn apart by glass. With amazing fortitude, John gathered up his broken family and amidst the confusion of the aftermath, he got them out of the rubble of their home.

John then managed to get his family onto a horse-drawn wagon, which took them all to the Cogswell Street Military Hospital where their wounds were dressed by a soldier and Georgina's injuries were stitched. From there they were taken to the Halifax Ladies' College, located at the corner of Harvey and Barrington Streets, where a temporary hospital had been set up to treat the severely injured. Eric was crying and had to be restrained while he was being examined by the doctors. Glass shards were removed from Eric's face and neck and his lacerations were stitched, but his eyes would have to be examined by a surgeon.

His parents stood by helpless, unable to relieve his pain or provide comfort to him. He suffered miserably until a doctor was able to administer sedation. Marjorie cowered under the metal examination table as she listened to Eric crying above her with her mother begging the doctors to ease his pain.

Shortly after arriving at the Ladies' College, baby Eric was examined by Dr. Arthur E. Doull, a Halifax eye, ear, and nose specialist. Dr. Doull determined that Eric's eyes were too damaged to save. Too many glass shards had penetrated them. Georgina and John were overwhelmed with sorrow when they were told that Eric's beautiful blue eyes would be removed. Any

Halifax Ladies' College where a doctor surgically removed Eric's eyes on December 6, 1917. Eric and his family remained there for a month while Eric recovered from his surgery.

hope they had that Eric's eyes could be mended was dashed. That very day Dr. Doull surgically removed both of Eric's eyes.[4] The eye muscles and remaining orbital contents were left intact so that Eric could eventually be fitted with artificial eyes when his sockets had healed sufficiently. The medical term for the removal of an eye is enucleation. Eric had a double enucleation. He would never see again.

There were a disproportionately large number of eye injuries resulting from the Halifax Explosion as so many people had stood at their windows watching the *Mont Blanc* burning in the harbour that morning. It was the largest mass blinding in Canada's history, and for that reason the Halifax Explosion was a paramount factor in the founding of the Canadian National Institute for the Blind (CNIB) in 1918. Approximately six hundred people suffered penetrating eye injuries and some degree of vision loss from flying glass.[5] Of this number, thirty-seven survivors were left completely sightless. Many survivors lost one eye, but only eighteen survivors had both eyes removed and six of them were children.[6]

4  NSARM RG14, Series S, vol. 17, School for the Blind, Correspondence and Medical Records re Eye Injuries from the Halifax Explosion.
5  Fraser Harris Report NSARM MG36, Series C, vol. 119.
6  NSARM RG14, Series S, vol. 17, School for the Blind, Correspondence and Medical Records re Eye Injuries from the Halifax Explosion.

--- DOUBLE ENUCLEATIONS. ---

| NAME | AGE | ADDRESS | OCCUPATION | DOCTOR |
|------|-----|---------|------------|--------|
| Apwood, Mrs.Geo. | 35 years. | 1 Pine St. | Housewife. | McLennan |
| Bardsley, John. | 27 " | 413 Agricola St. | Carpenter. | Y.M.C.A. |
| Conrod, Mrs. Victoria. | 30 " | 220 Longard Rd, | Housewife, | Y.M.C.A. |
| Davidson, Eric. | 3 " | 24 North Park St. | | Doull. |
| Dumaresq, Mrs. | 31 " | Ship Harbor. | Housewife. | V.G.H. |
| Dumaresq, Vera. | 9 " | " " | School girl. | V.G.H. |
| Griswell, Rita | 16 " | 39 John St. | " " | Y.M.C.A. |
| Heato, Mrs. Chas. | 26 " | Dartmouth. | Housewife. | N.S. Hos. |
| Hinch, Tommy. | 6 " | 104 Allen St. | School boy. | Childrens F |
| Hunt, Harvey. | 32 " | Commons, | Grocer. | Dr |
| Kearns, Clara. | 23 " | 140½ Creighton, | Housework. | C.H.Hosp. |
| Pitt, Tilly, | 52 " | St. Theresa Home. | " | Y.M.C.A. |
| Potter, Mrs. Harry. | 20 " | Morris St. Hosp. | " | Dr. Kirkpat |
| Stokes, Allen | 8 " | 104 Allen st. | School boy. | St. M.C.H. |
| Stokes, Mrs. John. | 45 " | 104 Allen St. | Housewife. | Infirmary. |
| Sutherland, Mary. | 6 " | 29 Chestnut St. | School girl. | Y.M.C.A. |
| Simmons, Francis. | 5 " | 32 Bishop St. | " " | C. Hosp. |
| White, Mrs. Katherine. | 34 " | 102 N. Park. | Housewife. | Dr. Schwart |

A list of survivors who had both eyes surgically removed following the Explosion.

At two and a half years of age, Eric Davidson was the youngest survivor of the Halifax Explosion to have both eyes surgically removed.

While the family was most fortunate to escape with their lives, Georgina's brother Maurice was not so lucky. His wife and his two young children died when their Acadia Street house collapsed. In a flash, his family was gone.

An unusual proposal about one year before the Explosion could have spared Eric from the tragic loss of his eyesight. Eric's Aunt Mabel and Uncle James Davidson in Winnipeg had two daughters but no sons and they very much wanted to have a little boy. When Eric was an infant, they offered to take Eric to live with them. Naturally, Eric's parents refused to let him leave, but if they had he may have been safely living in Winnipeg when the Explosion occurred.

# Recovery and Transition

I have no recollection of the Explosion. My sister was badly scalded. My mother suffered severe cuts to her body and almost bled to death. My father, who was on his way to work at the time, was blown against a tree and suffered severe hearing loss. But we survived the ordeal and made a new life for ourselves.[7]

Although Georgina lost a lot of blood, she suffered no permanent physical injury other than scarring from her lacerations. Marjorie's only injury was minor scalding burns, so she was easily treated. John was treated for minor abrasions and he had both of his eardrums blown out by the Explosion. He suffered permanent hearing loss but no other serious physical damage, which was remarkable given that he had been violently thrown through the air and into a tree.

While Georgina, John, and Marjorie did not require hospitalization, Eric needed to remain in hospital for several weeks. Bandages were wrapped around his tiny head to cover his empty eye sockets and everything was in darkness for him. He was terrified and did not want anyone to touch him except his mother. He cried for her and fussed when nurses changed his

---

7  Eric Davidson quoted in. H. Shea, "He's Not Just Any Mechanic," *The Atlantic Advocate*, 1988.

# HALIFAX RELIEF COMMITTEE.

NO. 1799   SECOND REGISTRATION   (DATE) Jan. 12 1918

| Surname | Address | No. of Rooms | Rent |
|---|---|---|---|
| Davidson, | At present. (Give exactly) 584 Gottingen St. Dec. (Dr. Jakeman) | 5 | 17.00 |

Block 3 Apt 26 North Park St

| First name | Age | Occupation | Weekly Earnings | Physical condition | Birth place and race Halifax. Years in — |
|---|---|---|---|---|---|
| 1. Man John Wm. | 35 | Clerk | $17.50 | ear drums blown out | England 25 |
| Wife 2. Woman Georgina | 32 | | | | Nova Scotia 5 |

| 3. Children | Age | Condition | LOSSES | Description | Estimated value |
|---|---|---|---|---|---|
| 4. John Eric | 2½ | badly burned badly injured and two eyes out | House (owned) Business (plant) Furniture and clothing Injury to health | Farm all destroyed. all very badly injured. | |
| 5. | | | | | |
| 6. | | | | | |
| 7. | | | | | |
| 8. | | | | | |

| Others in household s.19(1) | Relationship | RESOURCES | Kind. |
|---|---|---|---|
| | | Insurance amount? $1000.00 | Life |
| | | In what companies? Own Life (Mr. Somers | |
| | | Savings: amount? What bank? | |
| | | Real estate: value | |
| | | Location? | |
| | | Anything else? | |

What help has family received? Clothing. Food.

What are bread-winners doing? not able to work

Name of employers: Capt. Webb. Dockyard.
Present addresses

Is work permanent? Yes.

Employers before the fire of Present address
Capt. Webb. (Dockyard.)

PLANS FOR FUTURE
Family's estimate on what it needs and its plans:
Household utensils, dishes of all kinds. furniture, bedding blankets. etc. cooking stove.

How long does family expect to need help
in food? in shelter? in other ways?

Other references Present address
Rev. C. Crowdis.

Name of Church, Union, or other organization to which any member of family belongs
Grove Presbyterian.

Relatives: Name, Address,

Investigator's suggestion as to what should be done:
This is a very needy case all are under the doctor's care. Husband not able to work for sometime. please attend to this case at once.
Ability to help

Inquiries and dates:

C/ McLelland Investigator.

Halifax Relief Commission standard registration form for survivors of the Halifax Explosion. It briefly details Eric's family's injuries and the need for urgent attention.

bandages or attended to him. John and Georgina were anguished and wished to ease Eric's suffering as much as possible.

A conflict arose early on between Georgina and the Halifax Relief Commission's rehabilitation department when Georgina insisted on staying with Eric in the hospital. She would not be separated from him nor would she be separated from Marjorie. She had suffered unimaginable trauma from the Halifax Explosion and had very nearly lost both of her children. She was adamant that she not be apart from either of them now. She fervently maintained her position and the family was permitted to stay together at Ladies' College Hospital from December 6, 1917, until January 1, 1918.

The family was then transferred to Bellevue Hospital, which was another temporary hospital set up after the Explosion. While in hospital, Georgina's injured arm became infected and there was the possibility that she might lose her arm. She religiously bathed her arm in scalding water and it eventually healed on its own. On January 6, 1918, the doctors felt that Eric could be discharged into his parents' care. Eric's empty eye sockets had healed, but how long would it take for him to adjust to his new life without sight?

Miraculously, Georgina did not go into early labour or lose her baby following the Explosion, as so many pregnant women living within the disaster zone did. However, another conflict arose when Relief Commission rehabilitation personnel wanted to confine Georgina to a maternity ward away from her family, which was the custom at that time. Once again, Georgina would not be separated from Eric and Marjorie. She fought to keep them with her as noted in the Halifax Relief Commission report dated January 5, 1918:

"Mrs. Davidson is very bitter in her attitude towards the whole situation, would not consent for Eric to be away from her for some years to come."[8]

During these early days, Halifax Relief Commission social workers were mostly volunteers who were doing their best to deal with the massive workload of cases in the aftermath of the Explosion. While commission personnel may have found Georgina difficult, she was acting as many mothers who had suffered a traumatic ordeal would act. Georgina knew

8 M. R. Wilson, Halifax Relief Commission, Social Service Report, Halifax, 1918.

her family was lucky to be alive and that they had somehow survived the Explosion together when so many others had not. She feared separation from her children under any circumstances. In the end, Georgina was permitted to stay with her family and she was not confined to a maternity hospital. Her fierce maternal attachment to Eric and Marjorie forged in those early days following the Explosion would endure for the remainder of her life.

While many displaced survivors went to live with relatives in Nova Scotia and beyond, Eric's family remained in Halifax. John, Georgina, and the children moved four times in the first two years following the Explosion. Upon their discharge from Bellevue Hospital in January 1918, the family lived as refugees with Dr. William Jakeman, a Halifax veterinarian, at his home at 1 Doyle Street for two weeks before moving to a small bungalow in Rockingham for the remainder of the winter. Halifax Relief Commission documents refer to survivors as "refugees." While we in Canada think of refugees as displaced persons who come to Canada from war-torn countries, the Halifax Explosion created thousands of refugees in a flash. Eric's family were refugees for they were homeless and lost everything when their house collapsed.

In February 1918, John returned to his job at the HMC Dockyard. His employer had held his job for him and had generously continued to pay him a salary while he was recuperating with his family.

At the end of March 1918, when the temporary apartments on the Garrison Grounds were ready, the family moved to North Park Street from Rockingham. The Relief Commission rented these accommodations to the refugees; it was not free housing.

In April 1918, Georgina delivered a healthy baby boy, James. She was an incredibly strong woman to carry a healthy child to full term following the Explosion. Georgina received assistance from the Halifax Relief Commission in May and June 1918 to hire someone to help her after the birth of James, as is noted below.

Relief Commission report for May 17, 1918:

Delivered cheque for $20.00 in lieu of cash allowance for one month, May 15-June 15 to Mrs. Davidson. Mrs. Davidson was very grateful and said to thank Dr. Cutten.

In August 1918, the commission agreed to pay fifteen dollars a month to Eric's parents for the additional costs that his care incurred for a one-year period only. The commission would continue to pay any medical costs associated with Eric's eye care, but the other payments would stop.

Relief Commission report of August 3, 1918:

> See order from Dr. Cutten dated Aug. 1st to pay Mrs. Davidson $15.00 per month beginning Aug. 1st for one year. Same to be charged to the account of her son Eric Davidson.

In May 1918, John and Georgina received a settlement of eight hundred dollars from the Halifax Relief Commission for the loss of their worldly possessions, including furnishings, clothing, and personal belongings. Also in May 1918, John submitted a claim for the permanent damage to his eardrums and Georgina submitted a claim for her injuries. Neither was granted an award or a pension.

Because Eric was a minor, his parents had to select either the pension or the one-off lump sum payment for his loss of vision. They wisely chose the pension but Eric would not receive any pension funds from the Relief Commission until he reached seventeen years of age. His parents did not understand why their child's pension was deferred while blinded Explosion survivors over seventeen were receiving one. They believed that Eric should receive his pension and that it should be kept in trust for him until he reached seventeen. They were incensed. In the first few years following the Explosion, John wrote many strongly worded yet eloquent letters to the commission begging for financial assistance and complaining about the unjust treatment he felt his son was receiving. He was relentless but ultimately unsuccessful.

In a final act of defiance, John even refused to pay the monthly rent to the Relief Commission for the family's temporary accommodations. He eventually capitulated and made payment, realizing he was fighting a losing battle. The relationship between John, Georgina, and the commission was abrasive from the beginning and it had become strained by the time one year had elapsed following the Explosion. It did not improve much over the next few years.

While they were grateful to have a roof over their heads, Eric's parents were unhappy with the temporary housing conditions. While they had once lived in a comfortable apartment in Richmond with family and friends nearby, they were now crammed into tight quarters with many other people, most of whom they did not know. They had been displaced and nerves were raw. John expressed his frustration in a letter he wrote on February 7, 1919, to Dr. G. B. Cutten, Director of Rehabilitation, Halifax Relief Commission. An excerpt from that letter reads, "Only today one of the boys living near our place deliberately kicked over the 'kiddy car' with which our little boy Eric was playing and broke it. Conditions are getting intolerable."

The family subsequently moved to 49 Rector Street into a small bungalow built for summer occupancy. Then in November 1919, they moved to 11 Cabot Place in the newly built Hydrostone neighbourhood that the commission was constructing.

Transitioning to a life without vision was monumental for Eric and his parents and the frequent moves in such a short time span made it more difficult for him. Each move meant that he had to become acquainted with his new surroundings and furnishings. The only way to familiarize himself was to feel his way around in order to learn the layout of each room. He was still a toddler and he did not understand why it was now always dark, so he frequently asked his parents to turn on the lights. It was difficult for them to watch Eric trying to adjust to his sightlessness.

Occasionally Eric would strike out in frustration when things did not go as he wanted. His parents suddenly found themselves raising a blind child and they had no natural ability or formal training to do so. They wanted Eric to be happy, so John and Georgina pampered him and often allowed him to get away with behaviour that was not acceptable; they felt some misplaced guilt for Eric's condition, as parents often do when their child is injured.

There was no rehabilitation assistance or training available for Eric or for his parents as there is now, one hundred years later. In July 1918, a social worker advised Georgina how to care for and train a blind child in just two home visits. She also gave Georgina a booklet. That was the extent of the

#1799

FEB 8 1919

26 North Park St., Halifax, N. S.,
7th Feby, 1919.

Dr. G. B. Cutten,

   Rehabilitation Dept.;

     Halifax Relief Commission.

Dear Sir:-

     I would be glad to know if there is
any opportunity of getting a house in any part of the
City to live in, in the near future.

     Only to-day one of the boys living near
our place deliberately kicked over the "Kiddy Car" with
which our little boy Eric was playing and broke it.
Conditions are getting intolerable.

     I remain,

     Yours truly,

*Jack Davidson,*

Letter to the Halifax Relief Commission from Eric's
father, John. Eric's parents were anxious to move out
of temporary housing after living there for a year.

training. While Georgina was pleased to receive the booklet and the social worker's advice, she and John needed far more coaching and counselling for raising a child without eyesight. In time, the Halifax School for the Blind would offer these things but that was still a few years away.

Initially Eric did not want to leave his mother's side and he clung to her, fearing separation. Sounds were now extremely important to Eric and his hearing was becoming his keenest sense. Familiar voices comforted him. Sirens and strange noises terrified him. He was timid moving about and he was terrified of being alone in this new dark world.

One day a few months after the Explosion, a woman visiting Georgina urged Eric to leave his mother and walk across the room on his own to her. He refused. She then jingled a little bell and told Eric that if he walked over to her on his own she would give him the bell. This intrigued Eric. He took the bait and left his mother gingerly, making his way to the sound of the bell. That was the first time little Eric ventured away from his mother on his own. He was duly rewarded with the bell. These few steps were the beginning of his remarkable life of courageous steps forward relying upon sound. This visitor had no way of knowing how greatly she had contributed to his future independence.

In May 1918, Miss Lockwood, a field worker for the School for the Blind, reported that Eric was well and strong and that he played outdoors all day. She further noted that Eric was fond of music and that he had been given a Victrola, which he played himself. In July 1918, Miss Lockwood reported once again that Eric was well and strong and that he played outdoors most of the time. She also wrote that Georgina spoiled Eric absolutely, but that Eric was very bright and got around beautifully.

In October 1918, Dr. Doull noted that Eric's eye sockets were perfectly healed. He was not quite ready for artificial eyes yet, so eyeglasses were ordered for him.

Miss Lockwood visited regularly during the first two years following the Explosion to check on Eric's progress and she frequently took him for automobile rides. She noted in her reports that he enjoyed car rides and that he was well behaved when in her company, but she was concerned about his parents spoiling him.

October 26, 1918 report:

> Took Eric for a ride. Is very sturdy and bright. Goes around everywhere alone. Is very independent although extremely spoiled.

In June 1919, the topic of artificial eyes for Eric was put before his parents. He would need an operation on one of his lower eyelids and on each of his eye sockets. Georgina initially said no, as she was concerned about Eric being put through more surgery.  However, when it was explained to her that Eric needed these operations in order for artificial eyes to fit properly, she consented.

Over the next few years, Eric had operations on each of his eye sockets and on the one lower eyelid that was causing problems. In addition to these operations, Dr. Doull recommended that Eric's tonsils and adenoids be removed urgently, a procedure he carried out in May 1920. In the few short years since the Explosion, little Eric had undergone several operations.

Learning how to eat and drink without vision was another hurdle Eric had to overcome. Teaching him how to eat was challenging for Eric's parents too. He was only two and a half when he lost his sight so he was only just beginning to eat foods by himself, using utensils, before the Explosion. At three years of age, he had to learn to feed himself without sight. Eric struggled with foods like soups, finding it difficult to manage a spoon, which meant his parents had to feed him such foods initially. Solid foods like sandwiches were much easier. When he had a variety of food, such as a supper plate complete with meat and vegetables, he often had to feel the food to find it on his plate. When Eric started school at the Halifax School for the Blind, he learned to eat food on his plate using the twelve hours on the face of the clock. For example, vegetables may be at three o'clock, potatoes at six to nine o'clock, and meat, fish, or chicken at twelve o'clock. This method for locating food allowed Eric to eat his meal without drawing attention to himself in the company of sighted persons.

Like all toddlers, Eric was eager to dress himself. He learned quickly to button his shirts and pants. His clothing and shoes were placed where he could easily find them. Georgina still interceded to help Eric dress whenever she could. She constantly coddled him.

While John was struggling to pay the rent and feed and clothe his family following the Explosion, Georgina was finding it difficult to care for their children. Having a child without vision demanded a great deal of Georgina's attention and, like any child, Eric wanted to play outside with his siblings and the neighbourhood children. However, Georgina was anxious about letting Eric outside to play unattended. She worried that he may injure himself and she wanted someone with him whenever she could not be. She was worrying needlessly, it would seem, because Relief Commission reports from October 1918 indicate that Eric was robust and going everywhere on his own. Nevertheless, Georgina was becoming run down caring for her little family. Time and again, Georgina and John found themselves writing to the commission begging for financial aid to hire a girl to help with Eric. The constant fretting was beginning to take its toll on Georgina, as evidenced in an excerpt from a letter dated January 14, 1919, addressed to Dr. George B. Cutten, Director of Rehabilitation:

As there is more than a year elapsed since little Eric was injured and I have taken care of him as well as doing my work. It is more than I have strength for any longer so [I] am writing to ask you for assistance in taking care of Eric. He is growing and wants to be outside playing most of the day. This is natural and to be expected of course but he must have someone with him all the time and I find it impossible to do the both as much as I have tried. We will have to have a girl to take care of Eric and help him until he is able to take care of himself. When he is old enough for school we will only send him during school hours and have him brought home after school just like the other children. Even though he is blind he is the same dear little boy to me.

In addition to their efforts to cope with Eric's injury, his parents were themselves suffering mentally following the Explosion. Little was known about trauma-related mental illnesses at that time. Furthermore, there was no grief counselling following such tragedies as there is today. Most survivors carried the pain of that fateful day with them forever. Eric's parents were no different and, like most survivors of the Halifax Explosion, they did not care to talk about it. Furthermore they realized that there were many who suffered far more than they did. Georgina and John suffered in silence and grieved privately. This was similar to a festering sore and it only got worse.

In November 1919, almost two years after the Explosion, Georgina wrote to the Halifax Relief Commission again asking for assistance with caring for her children. In that letter her anguish is evident: "I have had nothing but sorrow since the time my dear boy lost his pretty eyes, or never shall be happy again but I do want to make Eric as comfortable as possible, dear boy. I miss him more than if he were dead."

At the same time, Eric's father was trying to cope as best he could. After work each day, he would bring Eric a small treat or toy even though the family was struggling financially. A letter from the commission dated September 21, 1918, admonished John for seeking financial assistance and spoiling Eric: "If as Mrs. Davidson informed us you never return home in the evening without bringing some gift for the boy ranging in value from twenty-five cents to seventy-five cents, this alone would meet the rent requirement and would save the risk of spoiling the child by unnecessary coddling."

While John was not being financially responsible by buying gifts for Eric, it was his way of coping with the situation that he suddenly found himself in. Because he knew Eric was captivated by cars, John managed to secure a Kiddie Car ride-in toy for Eric to sit in and pedal as he played outside. He knew it was extravagant but he wanted to see his little boy happy, and that in turn gave him some comfort.

John spent a great deal of time with Eric. He took Eric with him whenever he had the opportunity in order to teach him about his surroundings and to help Eric examine tactile objects and learn about the world around him. He even took Eric to examine the sites of many of the Richmond ruins in the years following the Explosion. One particular outing was a visit to the Richmond School site where he helped Eric physically examine the school ruins, explaining how children and teachers had died there. Another time they visited the ruins of Grove Presbyterian Church, and Eric examined with his hands the remains of the organ as it lay exposed to the elements. John often took Eric to the Wanderers Grounds too, when there were sporting events taking place, and Eric played on the junked cars stored there after the Explosion. John recognized that Eric had a keen interest in automobiles and he was eager to oblige his son and encourage him in this regard.

On June 16, 1919, John wrote to the Relief Commission asking for their assistance to secure an old junked car for Eric to play with in their backyard.

> I wonder if I may ask you if it would be possible to secure an old motor car of any kind that is ready for the junk pile for our little boy Eric to play with. As perhaps you know he is extremely fond of motor cars and I thought it might be possible to get an old car that was of no use to anyone and put it in the yard for him to amuse himself with this summer. Last summer when living on the south common I was in the habit of taking him to the Wanderers Grounds when there were any games on and as there were several old cars stored there since the Explosion that did not seem to belong to anybody he would play with the old cars for hours and they were a great source of enjoyment for him. Could not one of these cars be secured? I do not know whom to apply to so thought I would write you in the hope that you may be willing to assist us in this respect. We will greatly appreciate anything you may do for Eric in this matter.

A letter of response dated June 21, 1919, from the director of rehabilitation of the Halifax Relief Commission stated: "Your letter has been received but we regret we have no motor cars at our disposal and do not know of anyone who has."

While John was not successful in securing one of the old cars, it would seem that Eric's path to becoming an auto mechanic was set at a very tender age.

In 1920 the family grew with the birth of Walter and in 1923 a daughter, June, was born. Georgina and John now had five children. Their family was complete.

In 1921, when new homes were being constructed in Richmond, the family moved to 48 Rector Street. The frequent moves had been stressful for Eric and for his parents but now they could finally settle down.

That same year, United Memorial Church was completed and the family attended services at the newly constructed church with their surviving friends and family. John returned to singing in the choir and Marjorie and Eric attended Sunday school.

Six years after the Explosion, in 1923, Eric's eye sockets had healed and he was fitted with artificial eyes. The prostheses would require replacement from time to time, and the commission covered the cost of each replacement and any associated medical costs. Eric was still too young to cleanse his eye sockets or to place the eyes in them each morning or remove them as was required each night. His parents did this for him. Each day, they cleansed his eye sockets using cotton balls soaked in a solution of warm water and borac acid. Borac acid (a commonly used antiseptic in the early 1900s.) It would be some years before Eric would be able to look after these things himself.

Eric adjusted quickly to his sightlessness in those first years and he was so young when he lost his sight that he did not suffer mental trauma. Their response to Georgina's fateful dream before the Explosion and the trauma they experienced on December 6, 1917, would, however, affect John and Georgina for the rest of their lives. They blamed themselves for Eric's blindness and this placed a strain on their marriage. The memory of the house collapsing in upon her and the children and Eric's horrible injuries took a tremendous toll on Georgina and she was a changed woman. She lamented over Eric's blindness for the rest of her life, never fully recovering from the nightmare that was the Halifax Explosion.

In a letter to the Halifax Relief Commission in 1937, twenty years after the Explosion, Georgina wrote about her ongoing health issues, which she believed were the result of the disaster. One sentence exposes her mental suffering and her still-present grief over her son's loss of eyesight.

"Believe me I haven't had a days happiness since my son was injured."

She was subsequently examined by Dr. John G. MacDougall, chair of the commision's medical board. Dr. MacDougall determined that Georgina's physical injury complaints were subjective in nature. He did, however, report that Georgina displayed a marked psychoneurosis, which appeared to increase with age. The dictionary definition of psychoneurosis is a mental disorder that causes a sense of distress and deficit in functioning. Neuroses are characterized by anxiety, depression, or other feelings of unhappiness or distress. Dr. MacDougall's assessment of Georgina's mental condition would appear to confirm that Georgina indeed suffered from what is now known as post-traumatic stress disorder. While the Relief Commission was aware that survivors suffered mental injury from the Explosion, it did not consider it a pensionable injury.

# School Days

When I was a youngster I ran, walked, swam, and skated with the kids in
my neighbourhood. I never considered myself blind or any different from
them, and they never really considered me any different.[9]

The Halifax School for the Blind was officially opened on August 1, 1871,
as a private school and it was the first residential school for the blind in
Canada. The school accepted visually impaired children from the four
Atlantic provinces. Children as young as five left their families to live at
the school for several years, returning to their homes only at summer and
Christmas breaks.

It was a fortunate circumstance that the School for the Blind was well
established in Halifax by 1917, as there were so many people who suffered
permanent eye injuries in the Explosion. Sir C. Frederick Fraser, founder
and superintendent of the school, immediately recognized that there were
children and people of all ages who would benefit from services that the
school could provide. In January 1918, Fraser submitted an advertisement in
the Halifax newspaper, asking people to make application to the school
for their children who were blinded or partially blinded in the Halifax
Explosion. Sir Frederick, who was himself without sight, was instrumental

---

9  Eric Davidson quoted in G. Kelly, "Public Becoming more Aware of and Helpful to Blind People," *Halifax Chronicle Herald*, 1984.

in ensuring that survivors who had suffered eye injuries received proper medical care and follow-up treatment. He arranged for free eye clinics to be held at the School for the Blind and he organized the Blind Relief Fund through the Halifax Relief Commission to treat and rehabilitate the visually impaired Explosion survivors.

Initially, Eric's parents wanted to move to Boston when everything was settled so that they would be close to the Perkins School for the Blind for Eric's rehabilitation and education. A Halifax Relief Commission report from early 1918 stated that Sir C. Frederick Fraser had taken a personal interest in Eric's case. He reached out to Eric's parents and assured them that the School for the Blind offered every resource that the Perkins School offered, and he encouraged them to reconsider a move to Boston. Sir Frederick convinced Eric's parents to stay in Halifax and to apply for Eric to attend the school. Accordingly, on January 15, 1918, John wrote to Fraser and humbly asked that consideration be given for Eric to attend the school.

> I beg leave to report to you that our little boy, John Eric Davidson, age 2 years 8 months lost both his eyes in the explosion 6th Dec and is totally blind. He happened to be standing at a window playing with a little toy on the glass, and the flying glass cut his face and eyes in a terrible manner so that his eyes had to be removed. The baby (Eric) seems intensely fond of music and never tires listening to the gramophone at the house here.

Fraser also felt that Eric would be eligible for the blind baby nursery at the school when he had fully recovered from his injuries. An interview was granted and Eric attended the School for the Blind with his mother. However, Eric wanted nothing to do with the nursery and while he was playing with toys at a small table he had a temper tantrum and overturned the table, spilling its contents on the floor. While Eric's behaviour was not acceptable, it was not uncommon for a child who was recently blinded and, as he was rarely disciplined at home, he acted out when frustrated. Even though Georgina was finding it difficult to care for Eric and her other children, she decided to keep Eric home. She felt that he was not ready to be separated from her and she definitely was not ready to let him go. Accordingly, Eric did not attend the blind baby nursery.

For a period of time, John and Georgina refused to send Eric to school unless he could come home to them each day and they further requested that he be driven to and from school. Their expectation was beyond the limits of acceptability. However Sir Frederick took a keen interest in Eric and was concerned for his education and his future. Accordingly, Sir Frederick consented to provide a drive to school for Eric on Mondays and a drive home on Fridays but Eric would be a boarder from Monday to Friday. This was a most generous concession and it was agreed that Eric would begin school in September of 1920.

However, Georgina still wasn't ready to let go of Eric and over the next two years she was combative with the Relief Commission and with the school about a variety of things from Eric's school diet to who would take Eric's artificial eyes out each evening and put them in each morning at the school. Eric's parents were overly protective and they indulged him and gave him free reign. It was not a good situation.

Through the persistence of Sir Frederick and the Relief Commission rehabilitation department, Eric finally began his formal education at the School for the Blind, but not until 1922, at age seven. He was driven twice a week as promised, and he was a part-time boarder until he graduated. The drives were eventually removed and Eric then travelled on the streetcar with his mother or father.

As a weekly boarder, Eric's life became very different. At first, he was unhappy and he did not want to be away from his parents and his siblings. He particularly missed his mother. His school life was structured, which was something Eric was definitely not used to. Georgina too was having difficulty adapting to Eric being away from her and she was very critical of the care he received. If Eric showed any sign of illness during his first year at the school, Georgina pulled him, complaining that the school was not providing proper nutritional meals. The school staff worked with Georgina and eventually she began to cope better. It was a difficult time for all involved, especially Eric who did not do well academically until his parents were convinced that the school was where he needed to be and that they must stop disrupting his education.

Halifax School for the Blind where Eric received his formal education. Eric was one of the most successful graduates of the school. His wife, Mary, also attended the school where she excelled.

The school's education system had three departments: Literary, Music, and Manual Training. In the Literary department, the standard school courses from kindergarten to grade 12 were covered, including typewriting. Students were also taught how to read and write Braille, which is a raised system of points or dots for blind readers. Braille was a window to the world for the blind and therefore it was an imperative skill for the children to learn. The Music department provided training in piano music to all students. The school also provided some pipe-organ training and piano tuning for select students. Music examinations in theory and practice were taken by the students each year based on the Royal Conservatory of Music testing. Manual Training included woodwork, broom making, brush making, mattress making, shoe repair, chair caning, rug weaving, reed basketry, sewing, and knitting. Many of these trade classes would provide full- or part-time income for students after they graduated. In addition, there were physical drill classes taught by trained instructors. As the School for the Blind was a boarding school, a night watchman was employed to ensure the students' safety.

When the first bell rang at 7:15 in the morning, Eric got ready for breakfast and school along with the other children. Now a boarder, he slept in a dormitory with other boys. Girls and boys were not permitted to spend time together at the school. Eric was permitted to spend weekends and holidays with his family, which many of his classmates could not do. He made friends at the school and occasionally some of these friends were invited to spend a weekend at Eric's home with his family, which was a treat for them and Eric. The School for the Blind was a positive experience for Eric. He was learning new things and making new friends and it wasn't long before he began to enjoy his time there. He especially liked skating with the other children on the pond inside the school grounds in winter.

Following the morning physical exercise regime, the boys went to the assembly hall, sang hymns, recited the Lord's prayer, and heard Sir Frederick read from his own written books on nature and birds. Sir Frederick's stories planted the seed in Eric for what became a lifetime appreciation for nature, particularly the sounds of nature. Then it was off to their classrooms where Eric was taught mathematics, spelling, geography, history, and all the standard curriculum studies that sighted children were learning at that time.

Sighted people learn through visual images. The human brain takes a mental snapshot and stores it in the memory. Someone who has been blind all of their life does not have mental images to call upon as a sighted person does. Therefore, learning the alphabet and how to form letters and numerals, mathematics, and so on for which there is no mental image is challenging for someone without sight. As Eric was only two and a half years old when he lost his sight, he did not have a visual repository of memories.

At school, Eric learned to read and write Braille and he also learned how to print letters and numerals and cursive writing. His handwriting eventually became more legible than that of some sighted people.

The most important skill that Eric learned at the school was independence. He learned how to navigate around barriers and how to walk along Halifax sidewalks and streets, using a white cane and his acute hearing to guide him. Sometimes he even went without his cane. There were challenges for sure and he did have his fair share of missteps.

One day when Eric was approximately eleven, he decided to venture away from school on his own. He wanted to test his ability to walk about the streets without supervision, so he didn't tell anyone at the school what he was up to. He headed toward Barrington Street, which was several blocks east of the School for the Blind. He walked east along South Street with the sounds from the harbour guiding him along. Eric safely made his way beyond Barrington Street to Water Street, which runs along the harbour waterfront. He then headed north along Water Street for a few blocks but when he tried to head back to the school he became disoriented. A policeman on patrol noticed Eric was having difficulty and asked him where he was trying to go. Eric explained that he was attempting to return to the School for the Blind. The policeman flagged a man driving a horse-drawn laundry cart and instructed the man to take Eric back to the school several blocks away. Eric was so embarrassed that day that he vowed he would never get lost again. In time, his knowledge of Halifax city streets would become one of his many remarkable talents.

In a few years, Eric became one of the senior boys at the school, and it was up in the morning, a cold shower, a run around the block, and off to the gym for a workout. The workout involved using dumb bells, parallel bars, rings, and matt-work under the supervision of a qualified instructor. Eric was an eager participant in sports and physical activities both in and outside of the school.

Eric developed a habit of leaving without telling anyone at the school where he was going. His headstrong attitude must have caused his supervisors some anxious moments from time to time. One of his adventures found him and his pal Roy Kelly stepping out by themselves. Like Eric, Roy was completely without sight. The two boys walked south on Tower Road toward Point Pleasant Park. There were and still are railway tracks that run beneath Tower Road. However, to get to those train tracks below involves a treacherous climb down a steep embankment. Not something any sighted person should undertake let alone two lads with no sight at all. The embankment from top to bottom is approximately twelve metres in height. Eric and Roy could have fallen and hurt themselves quite seriously, but somehow they both managed to crawl safely to the bottom. Once they were at the bottom though, a railway worker spotted them along the tracks and shouted at them to get out of there. They scrambled back up the embankment again without injury, an amazing feat. Once they were at the top, the two boys hooted and hollered. They enjoyed the thrill of the adventure and were quite proud of themselves as they made their way back to the school and possible repercussions. Two curious young boys looking for a bit of adventure, not unlike what any sighted boy their age would be doing.

On another adventure, the two friends decided to go for a skate on the frog pond at Point Pleasant Park, which was several blocks south of the school along Tower Road. They would have been roughly twelve years old as they walked south on Tower Road. They easily made their way to the frog pond, donned their skates, and then skated without restriction on the frozen pond. What a feeling of freedom it gave them to be skating on their own. At that time there was a small Irish community aptly called Irishtown in South End Halifax. While skating at the pond that day, a young Irish girl befriended Eric. They held hands and skated around the pond together. Eric was infatuated and thought he was in love. This was the first girl who had ever shown him any such attention and he considered her to be his first ever girlfriend. He returned to the frog pond many times hoping to skate again with the Irish girl but never met her again.

Eric was a scamp and he was always looking for ways to have a bit of fun. On more than one occasion, he and Roy would get up early and covertly make their way to the front steps of the school. Once there, they helped themselves to the milk, which had been delivered to the school minutes before and left unguarded on the steps. Amazingly, they were never caught. In 1927 when Eric was twelve, the school's boys went on strike for better quality food. There was lots of food at the school but the boys felt it was poorly prepared. The plan was that all the boys would refuse to eat their dinner and create a stir in the dining room. When the time came for the strike though, only one boy carried through.

Eric's most serious infraction at school was in 1929 when he was caught smoking by one of the instructors. Eric was only fourteen. The school promptly informed Eric's parents of this misdemeanour. After several years of dealing with Eric's parents, it should have come as no surprise to school officials that his parents responded by saying that they approved of Eric's smoking. In truth, his parents did not approve of Eric smoking but they had difficulty admitting that to the officials. The school duly reported to the Relief Commission rehabilitation department that Eric's parents' response to his smoking accounted for Eric's lack of enthusiasm academically. Halifax School for the Blind report cards in those days were either handwritten or typed on a plain piece of paper and signed by the principal. Eric's report cards reveal that he was an average student.

A class that Eric enjoyed was woodworking. He learned how to do basic carpentry tasks and he excelled in this class. He subsequently put these newly learned skills into practice at home by building a ride-on wooden train complete with the tracks in his backyard. His parents were happy to oblige Eric with his carpentry and provided the materials for this and other projects he attempted. Conversely, shoe repair was a class that Eric did not excel at. In fact, one day while repairing a shoe he cut the whole top off the shoe.

Making brooms was another class Eric did not enjoy, but when the instructor of the broom department asked him if he would like to earn some money selling brooms, Eric was delighted at the prospect. The brooms cost forty-nine cents and Eric could earn twenty-five cents for each broom he sold. He was keen to earn some money so he eagerly set out to sell brooms. However after walking the streets of downtown Halifax all afternoon without selling a single broom, Eric was deflated.

Eric learned to play the piano at the School for the Blind. But he wanted to learn to play a banjo, which was not an instrument taught there. Eric's parents, who had noted his fondness for music when he was a small child, encouraged him. They purchased a banjo for him and like many things Eric would come to do in his life, he taught himself how to play on his own. Eric had a sharp ear for music and he strummed his banjo at every opportunity. He easily recognized when strings needed replacement and he replaced them himself, identifying the gauge of each string by touch. He was a natural musician.

When he was about thirteen, Eric decided that it was time for him to travel home from school on the streetcar by himself. His determination and his independence were beginning to emerge. No one was more anxious than Georgina about this decision. She was watching as Eric, determined to succeed, marched briskly along Rector Street with his back straight and his head held high. That first ride home on the streetcar at such a young age was a major accomplishment for him. He was thrilled at his newfound

SCHOOL FOR THE BLIND.   Pupils' Record.   Spring Term, 1929.

*Eric Davidson — Grade Five.*

| | | | |
|---|---|---|---|
| Deportment | 79 | Algebra | — |
| Braille Reading | 70 | Geometry | — |
| Print Reading | — | French | — |
| Braille Writing | | Latin | — |
| Print Writing | 30 | Piano | 65 |
| Spelling | 85 | Piano Tuning | — |
| English | 68 | Woodwork | 78 |
| Geography | 17 | Chair-seating | 70 |
| History | 48 | Shoe Repair | — |
| Science | — | Physical Drill | 62 |
| Arithmetic | 69 | | |

SCHOOL FOR THE BLIND.   SUMMER EXAMINATIONS. 1929.

Pupil's Name *Eric Davidson.*   Grade *Five*

| | | | |
|---|---|---|---|
| Deportment | 85 | Arithmetic | 33 |
| Braille Reading | 60 | Algebra | — |
| Print Reading | — | Geometry | — |
| Braille Writing | 45 | French | — |
| *Print Writing* 30 Spelling | 60 | Latin | — |
| English | 60 | Piano | 66 |
| Geography | 15 | Organ | — |
| History | 50 | | — |
| Science | — | Wood Work | — |
| Physical Drill | 67 (67) | Chair Seating | 65 |

Eric's grade-5 report cards from the Halifax School for the Blind in 1929. Eric often said he did not like geography and his report card appears to confirm that.

independence and had proven to himself and to his family that he could travel by himself on public transportation. This was just the tip of the iceberg for his lifetime of incredible achievements.

Eric left the School for the Blind when he was seventeen. It had been fifteen years since he had lost his sight and he had grown from a headstrong and somewhat pampered child into an independent young man capable of looking after himself. The School for the Blind had been paramount in Eric's development, for it was at the school that he learned to conquer his fears and to adapt to living without sight.

While his parents overindulged Eric, they did their best to give him a normal, happy childhood given the circumstances they had so tragically found themselves in. They encouraged Eric in whatever interest he had, whether it was music or his dream of a career in automobile mechanics. So with the skills he acquired at the school and with his parents' support, Eric matured into a confident young man. Now he was eager to strike out on his own like other young men his age.

Eric Davidson would soon become one of the most successful and well-known graduates of the Halifax School for the Blind.

# Defying the Odds

I always wanted to be a mechanic. I used to think about that often, wondering if anyone would ever give me a chance.[10]

From early childhood, Eric knew that he wanted to be an automobile mechanic. So upon completing his education at the School for the Blind in 1932, Eric attempted to enrol in an automobile mechanic course at the Nova Scotia Technical College. He was turned down because of his visual disability.

The registrar told Eric that he didn't think it was safe for him to take the course because he was blind. Eric then requested to meet with the principal who was concerned that the young student might lose a finger or otherwise injure himself. The principal suggested to Eric that he should learn to fix washing machines instead because no one would hire a blind mechanic. Eric responded that he could just as easily lose a finger fixing washing machines.

While the attitude of the registrar and the principal was cruel in nature, ignorance of physically challenged persons and their abilities was common in those days. Eric was humiliated as he left the Technical College that day but he did not allow this rejection to deter him. Quite the opposite. He would not give up on his dream, and he determined that this was an obstacle that he would have to find a way to overcome.

10 Eric Davidson quoted in Shea, "He's Just Not Any Mechanic," 1988.

Eric was tenacious. If he could not attend trade school then he'd just have to teach himself. When he received his first pension cheque from the Halifax Relief Commission in 1932, he used the entire cheque to buy a 1925 Chev. The car cost fifty dollars. His parents were eager to help him and accommodated by letting him use the backyard to work on the car. His entire family supported him. Eric purchased automobile manuals and his brothers Walter and Jim read them to him. His parents and sisters read the manuals to him too, but for the most part it was his brothers.

With the information Eric gleaned from the manuals, he experimented by taking the Chev engine apart and putting it back together over and over again in the backyard. When he got the engine working perfectly, he would disconnect something and listen to the difference in sound that the engine made. After many such disconnects and reconnects, he was able to pinpoint an engine's problem by listening to how the engine was running.

In addition to using his sense of hearing to establish mechanical issues, Eric also used his senses of touch and smell. He could readily smell a car burning oil so he removed the plugs and felt the points for carbon. If he was repairing a headlight or tail light, he felt the bulb and if it warmed up, it was on and working. He tested ignition coils and condensers by listening to the sound of the high-voltage spark they produced. He kept his hands clear of the fan belt and was extremely careful when working on a car while the engine was running.

Eric was determined to teach himself everything he could about auto mechanics. In time, he could take apart and repair vehicles with the speed and accuracy of sighted mechanics. Soon friends and neighbours began to bring their cars to Eric. The fact that they trusted him with their vehicle repairs was encouraging to him and he began to realize that he was making headway toward his dream.

There was only a few years' difference in age between Eric and his brothers, Jim and Walter, and as the boys grew up they were very close. In the winters, they enjoyed skating at Chocolate Lake in Armdale. Eric was a strong skater and he and his brothers enjoyed a good game of hockey using a tin can as a puck so that Eric could hear it and follow it. He liked to skate hard and fast whenever he had the opportunity and when he knew it was

Brothers Jim, Eric, and Walter with their dog, Towser, 1931. The boys were practically inseparable growing up.

safe to do so. In the summers, the boys went swimming in Halifax Harbour or drove out to Papermill Lake in Bedford. They drove the 1925 Chev everywhere, and in those days the roads were gravel so the ride was often quite dusty.

Sometimes, Eric would get behind the wheel of the car and drive with one of his brothers shouting out directions for him, "Go right, Eric, drive straight on, Eric, or hard left, Eric." Driving was a thrill for him. When gears had to be changed, his brother would take the wheel and steer while Eric shifted gears. Clam Harbour Beach on the Eastern Shore was a favourite spot for Eric to experience the thrill of driving his car. The empty beach gave him such a wonderful opportunity to handle a motor vehicle. Sometimes, he even took the wheel on north Gottingen Street in Halifax when no one was around. Always one of his brothers was with him for these thrill rides and always they ensured there was no danger to them or to anyone else. Eric did not drive unaccompanied on public roads.

Eric and Walter often took the Chev for long drives to Windsor, about thirty miles west of Halifax or to Kentville, sixty miles west of Halifax in the Annapolis Valley. Eric found the variety of smells that the countryside offered exhilarating, from the pleasant scent of freshly cut hay to the sharp aroma of manure. He especially liked to drive to the Valley in May when the fragrant apple blossoms were in bloom. In the fall when the apples were ready for picking, Eric and his brothers picked apples right from the tree. Eric's love of the Annapolis Valley began in the mid-1930s when he frequently stayed at the Whitman farm in Aylesford. The Whitmans were friends of the family and Eric took every opportunity he had to visit their farm. Staying in the country experiencing farm life was refreshing for him, as it was so different from life in the city. He was able to get close to and handle farm animals and he enjoyed the myriad of sounds that are typical on a farm.

On occasion, the boys would take girls for rides with them, Eric and his date sitting in the back and Walter or Jim and his date up front. On one of these dates Eric sensed that the girls were uncomfortable around him because of his blindness. This was confirmed when they stopped at a restaurant in Windsor and the girls ate by themselves at a separate table away from Walter and Eric. Eric felt dejected. He felt that no girl with sight would want to spend time with a blind man. Walter was annoyed at the girls' behaviour and he let them know as much in no uncertain terms. It was a quiet ride back to the city. While Eric would have preferred if Walter had said nothing, he knew why Walter had spoken to the girls. They were brothers and they looked out for each other. That was just how it was.

One cold winter day in 1934, Eric, Walter, and Jim were driving the Chev along Kempt Road when they picked up a hitchhiker carrying a guitar. The hitchhiker was Hank Snow. Hank Snow was a Nova Scotia man who became a famous country singer in Nashville in the late 1930s through to the 1960s. However in the early 1930s, Hank was not yet famous and he went by

Hank Snow performing in Halifax at the Halifax Forum in the 1980s.

his given name, Clarence Snow. He was living in Fairview, trying to eke out a living doing odd jobs and singing here and there. On this particular day, he was heading to the local Halifax radio station CHNS where he sang on a weekly program, *Clarence Snow and His Guitar.*

Eric and his brothers offered Hank a ride to the station and this chance encounter became a lifelong friendship between Eric and Hank. The boys drove Hank from Fairview to CHNS on several occasions and Hank was occasionally invited for dinner at the Davidson home, which was then on Kaye Street in North End Halifax. They had jam sessions with Eric playing banjo and Hank singing and playing guitar. In 1936, Eric and Hank recorded a song together at CHNS, "The Maestro with the Banjo." Hank often referred to Eric as "the maestro with the banjo."

Eric and Hank kept in touch over the years, communicating on reel-to-reel tapes, Hank in Nashville and Eric in Halifax. When Hank returned to Halifax in the 1960s, Eric and his family went to the Halifax Forum to see him perform. They were invited backstage after the show and the two old friends chatted and laughed together for some time until Hank had to leave. Hank never forgot the kindness that Eric and his brothers showed him in those early days and he mentioned the three Davidson brothers driving him to CHNS in his autobiography, *The Hank Snow Story*.

Eric was not employed after completing his schooling, so he continued to work on any car he could get his hands on and his brothers continued to read automobile manuals to him. When he turned twenty-one in 1936, the Halifax Relief Commission gave him one hundred dollars, as was the custom for the commission when children receiving a pension reached that age. He decided to sell the 1925 Chev and buy another car. Off to Windsor he went with his brothers and he bought a 1930 Buick. It was a sport touring car with a nickel radiator, nickel headlights, and even the gearshift and handbrake were nickel-plated. Eric was thrilled with his new car, which was a luxury for him and his brothers. The boys enjoyed showing off in the Buick, driving around town and taking girls for a spin here and there. Unfortunately, Eric's parents' home on Kaye Street did not have a garage for the Buick, so within a few years the nickel started weathering. Eric was disappointed that he was unable to prevent the car from deteriorating but he did keep the engine in top running order and he and his brothers used that car for many more years to come.

In the late 1930s, Eric worked for a short period of time for the Canadian National Institute for the Blind (CNIB) weaving reed bottle protectors for ships' bottles to prevent them from breaking on rough seas. Then he worked at the CNIB canteen at Halifax City Hall. All the while though, Eric remained intrigued with the mechanics of automobile engines and he never gave up on his dream of someday becoming a mechanic.

In 1942 while working in the canteen, Eric received the terrible news that his father had suffered cardiac arrest and passed away. His father was only sixty years old. Eric, who was extremely close to his father, was shattered. They had spent so much time together and his father had taught him so much. Eric and Marjorie were living at home still and now Eric felt it was his responsibility to support his mother. He would simply have to work harder at becoming a licensed mechanic. Eric soldiered on, tearing apart and rebuilding automobile engines in the backyard.

In 1944, things were about to change in Eric's life. An industrial-placement officer came by the canteen one day and asked Eric if he would like to try something else for a change. Eric told him about his dream to become a mechanic. The officer did not try to talk Eric out of his plan. He saw something special in Eric and he wanted to assist him in reaching his goal. Later that day, he returned to the canteen and told Eric that Citadel Motors at the corner of Brunswick and Sackville Streets had an opening and that the manager would like to speak with him. Eric could not believe his luck. He knew there was a shortage of workers because so many young men had gone off to the Second World War, but this was unexpected.

Eric was nervous but he mustered up the courage to walk into the dealership and apply for the position. Harold Robinson, the manager at Citadel Motors, expressed his concerns about Eric being able to find his way around the shop without getting hurt. They made a deal that if Eric could get around the shop on his own without bumping into anything, the job was his. Robinson then gave Eric a tour of the shop, indicating to him where obstacles such as tool benches and machines were located and where the vehicles would be parked. Eric then confidently walked through the shop on his own without his white cane, and without incident manoeuvred easily around jacks, stands, cars, and even a huge furnace. Eric had impressed Harold Robinson such that Harold took a leap of faith and hired him then and there as a mechanic's helper. Finally, someone was giving Eric the chance he had longed for. He was elated that he could now begin to officially work for his qualification papers. He was most grateful to both the placement officer and to Robinson for giving him this critical break.

Eric worked earnestly at Citadel Motors, a GM dealership. One of his jobs was installing heaters into new cars because the cars were shipped to the dealership without heaters. Eric was repairing a variety of vehicles on a daily basis and constantly learning and improving his skills. If that was not enough, he was getting paid to do what he truly enjoyed. He was thrilled to

Eric and co-workers at Citadel Motors Halifax, 1944 or 1945. Eric appears pleased to be standing next to the pretty female employee who has her arm draped over his shoulder.

go to work each day. Before long, the shop manager and the owner of Citadel Motors were both so pleased with Eric's work that they gave him permission to work on his own vehicle in the shop when the garage was closed for business. One evening, Eric was working on his car in the garage well after closing time. It was dark outside and a police officer patrolling the downtown area heard noises coming from inside. There were no lights on in the garage so the police officer thought there was a burglar inside. When he went inside to investigate, he found Eric working away on the car. There was quite a conversation about what was going on but Eric assured the officer he had permission to use the garage. The officer verified Eric's story by contacting the owner at home. When he was assured there was no burglary in progress and that Eric had permission to be in the garage, the policeman left to carry on his patrol. What a story that police officer must have related to his comrades later back at the station—imagine a blind man working on a car!

In 1948, Eric received his automobile mechanics licence from the Province of Nova Scotia. He had done it! He was now a licensed mechanic! Georgina and Eric's siblings were all extremely proud of him. Eric wished that his father had lived to see him earn his papers.

By 1948, men who had been overseas had returned to work and Eric eventually lost his job at Citadel Motors. Some of the veterans knew Eric and didn't want to see him lose his job so they refused work at Citadel if they were taking a job away from him. They admired Eric for what he had accomplished and they wanted to see him continue. Regardless, Eric had to move on, but coincidentally years later he would work with some of these very same men at the Halifax City Field garage. Eric harboured no hard feelings against his employer or the men returning to their jobs. Quite the opposite—he was thankful to have worked for four years at Citadel Motors and he was grateful to the veterans for their service overseas.

After leaving Citadel Motors, Eric went back to work for the CNIB. He was now an employment placement officer or recruiter, travelling by train throughout Nova Scotia and New Brunswick establishing jobs and career opportunities for blind persons in the Maritimes. He was comfortable with his position but he knew it wasn't what he wanted to do. He was a licensed mechanic and he wanted to work on cars so he continued to look for a job in his field while he was employed with the CNIB. He was also enjoying a very active social life with his brothers, going to socials and dances, and with his visually impaired friends at CNIB gatherings, dances, and bowling in mixed bowling leagues. He was a member of the Fraser Club, a social group of graduates from the Halifax School for the Blind, which held a Blind Bowling League at United Memorial Church on Kaye Street, where Eric's family also worshipped.

# A Love Match

In January 1948, while bowling with the Fraser Club mixed bowling league at the church, Eric met Mary Zinck. Mary was visually impaired and had attended the School for the Blind from 1930 to 1940. Eric and Mary were both at the school between 1930 and 1932 but Mary was five years younger so they really had not known each other then.

Mary was a remarkable woman in her own right and she faced many challenges in her young life too. She was born on a farm in the small rural community of Hebbs Cross, Lunenburg County. Mary was born with cataracts in both of her eyes because her mother had contracted rubella while she was pregnant. As a result, Mary had very limited vision in both of her eyes. When she was a little girl, a doctor in Bridgewater performed an operation on her right eye to remove the cataract. The operation was a disaster that left Mary with no vision at all in that eye. All that remained was the extremely limited vision she had in her left eye.

At ten years old, Mary left her home and her family to attend the School for the Blind in Halifax. Unlike Eric, who was able to return to his family on weekends, Mary would live at the school for roughly ten years, spending only summers, Christmases, and other school breaks with her family until she finished her schooling. Mary excelled at the School for the Blind, graduating with honours in 1940. In 1944, when she was twenty-four, Mary travelled alone to Boston for an operation on her left eye. That

Mary attended the School for the Blind in Halifax where she graduated with honours. This photo, taken in 1921 before Mary's arrival, shows a typical girls' class engaged in activities such as machine sewing, weaving, needlepoint, and knitting.

operation gave her slightly more vision. Mary was thrilled with even that little improvement. She would always be legally blind though, as the vision she now had in her left eye was still only in the vicinity of 10 percent. Mary decided to make a life for herself in Halifax where she had made many friends rather than return to her parents' home where she would be somewhat secluded and away from people her age. She got a job working in the concession stand at the Clayton Clothing Factory on the corner of Barrington and Jacob Streets and she rented a room on Tobin Street where she could walk to work.

Mary and Eric were both registered clients of the CNIB and in fact they were among the first clients of the CNIB after it came into existence in 1918. Eric became a CNIB client in March 1920 and Mary in February 1921.

After two nights of bowling together on the same team, Eric asked Mary out on a date. Their first date was a sleigh ride in the North End of

Halifax, sponsored by the CNIB Fraser Club. There were two sleighs full of visually impaired young people. Eric and Mary were sitting on the tailgate of the first sled and the horses that were pulling the second sled were practically touching them. In fact, the horses were so close that Eric and Mary could feel their breath as they clip-clopped along so Eric would yell at the horses to back off when they got too close. This carried on throughout the evening ride and they had a wonderful time together. Afterwards, they went to a downtown restaurant before Eric walked Mary home. This was the first of many dates to come.

Eric liked to impress Mary so he would often take her for rides in his 1930 Buick. This meant double dating with another couple, usually one of his brothers. Most of their dates though involved going for long walks in Point Pleasant Park and around Halifax; sometimes they even walked in raging snowstorms. Eric would meet Mary after work and walk her back to her rooming house on Tobin Street where the matron would be waiting for Mary's return. One night after they had been out on a date, Mary found herself locked out because she tarried a bit too long and had missed the curfew. Eric hammered on the door until the matron answered and he stayed there until he saw Mary safely inside. The matron was not pleased and blamed Eric for Mary's tardiness.

During their courtship, Eric had been looking for employment as an auto mechanic locally and as far away as Ontario. With a glowing letter of reference from Citadel Motors, Eric landed a job at Patterson Motors in Ottawa, a Chrysler Plymouth dealership, to start work on June 1, 1950. An excerpt from that letter reveals Eric's skill and quality of work.

While Mr. Davidson is sightless we found his work to be thoroughly satisfactory from a quality viewpoint and might say we had considerably less than average in the way of policy adjustments on mechanical operations which had been carried out by him. Once familiar with the layout of the shop, the lack of sight did not appear to be too great a handicap. As an employee we would recommend him as an excellent type, being always cheerful, industrious and co-operative with his fellow workers.

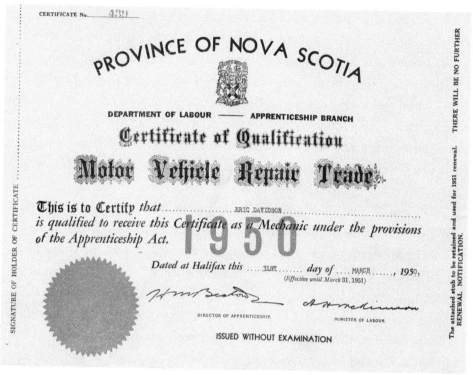

Eric's 1950 Nova Scotia mechanic's licence.

In the 1950s it was not common to hire a handicapped person, especially a man without sight for the position of mechanic. Like Harold Robinson at Citadel Motors, Mr. F. C. Patterson was a man ahead of his time.

Eric was now employed as a qualified and licensed vehicle mechanic so he decided it was time to ask Mary to marry him. While they were out on one of their evening strolls on May 26, 1950, Eric proposed on the bridge train tracks above Kempt Road in North End Halifax. Mary accepted Eric's proposal. Their courtship had lasted two years.

Eric left by train for Ottawa in early June. Mary followed in mid-August. In the meantime, they would have to correspond by way of Braille letters. An excerpt from one of Mary's letters to Eric, dated June 26, 1950:

> My dearest Eric, do you know dearest it is just a month today since we were engaged and the ring has not been off since you put it on. I look at it

so often and think of what you said when you put it on. Do you remember dearest?

In early August, Eric's letter to Mary:

Dear Mary, You will be leaving Halifax the 20th of this month I suppose. I don't know what train you are coming on. I would like to know so I can meet you. I will come to the station. I suppose this will be the last letter I write you before you leave. So long my Sweet for now. Good luck on your journey. Love Eric.

It took fortitude for Eric to leave his family and his Halifax home. Eric's knowledge of Halifax city streets exceeded that of most residents but he was not familiar with Ottawa streets. Yet, he was resolute and committed to succeed in his chosen career. He wanted to work as a mechanic and if he had to move to Ottawa to do so, then that is what he would do.

He had worked only a short time in Ottawa when word began to spread that there was a blind mechanic working at Patterson Motors. In due course, the *Ottawa Journal* ran the story "Eric Davidson, Doing Things The Hard Way." This was the beginning of what would become a lifetime of media focus on Eric Davidson and it marked the beginning of his celebrity.

Eric and Mary arranged to be married in Ottawa on August 25, 1950, by Reverend J. P. C. Fraser. As luck would have it though, Reverend Fraser had developed leg problems and could not stand. He had taken to his bed so Eric and Mary found themselves on their wedding day standing in the minister's bedroom exchanging their vows. This was most unusual but they were determined to be married. Their close friend Arch Rasley, who was also a survivor of the Halifax Explosion, and his girlfriend, Carmen Crotty, stood as their witnesses while they took their vows. Mary was thirty years old and Eric was thirty-five.

The reception was held at the home of Ella Hoy who was a close friend and the owner of the home where Eric and Mary lived in Ottawa. Their honeymoon was brief as Eric had to return to work a few days later, so they stayed at a cottage in Arnprior just outside of Ottawa. It was quaint but

Eric and Mary on their wedding day in Ottawa, August 1950.

they were happy. There was no kitchen in the cottage so they had to walk a fair distance to take their meals at a nearby home. A few months later, they managed to have a wonderful weekend away in Niagara Falls, even taking a ride on the *Maid of the Mist*. In early 1951, they moved to Toronto where Eric had secured a job at Port Credit Motor Sales at a higher rate of pay. Just as in Ottawa the year before, word spread about the blind mechanic. The media in Toronto sought Eric out for a story as well. Eric was modest and a little uncomfortable about this sudden notoriety.

Considering that Eric and Mary left Halifax to be married and that they were married unconventionally in a minister's bedroom, one might naturally think that their urgency to be married meant that they had to be married. That was not the case. It was a few months after their marriage that Mary realized she was pregnant. Mary and Eric were over the moon when they learned they were going to be parents. This was a dream come true for them both as they each grew up thinking there was a good possibility they may not marry or have children because of their visual handicaps. They knew they would face new challenges as parents but they also knew they were very capable of raising a family.

Their son John, named for Eric's beloved father, was born in August 1951. While Eric and Mary had planned to return to Halifax at some point, their desire to be back home was stronger than ever because they were now a family. So in 1952, with letters of reference from his Ottawa and Toronto employers, Eric and his little family returned to Halifax.

F. C. Patterson, owner and general manager of Patterson Motors in Ottawa, wrote Eric a letter of reference dated May 14, 1952. An excerpt from that letter reads:

….we found Mr. Davidson to be a very conscientious and willing worker, and while being physically handicapped he performed his duties without assistance in our shop….We were very sorry to lose the services of Mr. Davidson and highly recommend him to any garage operator.

T. A. Casey, service manager at Port Credit Motor Sales in Toronto stated in his letter of reference, dated May 5, 1952:

….it was a pleasure to watch Mr. Davidson operate. He does not require help after being shown where tools and equipment are kept.

Upon their return to Halifax, Eric rented space in a Rockingham garage and set up his own automobile-repair business. He walked to and from work each day, a total of four miles. While operating his own business gave him a feeling of pride, Eric was barely earning enough money to make ends meet. To make matters worse, some customers did not pay for the repairs when the work was complete, promising to return later with the payment but never doing so. Eric carried on but he knew he had to find another job. He could not support his small family this way. In the meantime, Mary and Eric desperately wanted to buy a house but wondered how they could swing it on Eric's salary. Mary was very clever and had a real way with finances so she came up with a plan.

They secured a small loan from the CNIB for a down payment and bought their first house at 27 Prescott Street in the North End. It was a small wood-frame storey-and-a-half with a single detached garage. While Mary and Eric lived in the downstairs, they rented the upstairs to a sighted couple who also happened to be their good friends. The rental income supplemented Eric's salary and his small monthly Relief Commission pension. Mary's creative financing enabled them to buy the house without worrying about how to meet their monthly mortgage commitment. Together, they overcame one of their first major hurdles as a married couple. They were proud homeowners.

Standing outside 27 Prescott Street working on his 1935 Rolls Royce, Eric gave his first television interview to CBC reporter J. Frank Willis on December 1, 1957, forty years after the disaster. The interview "Surviving the Disaster of the Halifax Explosion" is available online at CBC Archives.

It is a very poignant and moving interview. As well as interviewing Eric, Willis interviewed Billy Wells, who was driving the fire truck Patricia destroyed in the Explosion, and an unnamed older woman who was visually impaired and visibly shaken, wringing her hands as she retold her story.

# One of the Boys

In September 1954, Eric made application to the City of Halifax for a position as an auto mechanic in the City Field garage. Mary typed the letter on her Smith Corona typewriter and Eric signed it:

> I hereby wish to apply for the job as mechanic in the City Field garage. I have held my mechanic's license since 1948. From 1950 to 1952 I lived in Ontario at which time I worked and held my license in that province. The following years I have lived in the city of Halifax and have my license for this province. I am a married man with one child. Hoping you will give this application favourable consideration.

It was nearly a year later before he was called for an interview. George West, Commissioner of Works for the City of Halifax, was impressed with Eric who by now was gaining considerable notoriety for himself. George West, like Eric's previous employers, was a man ahead of his time and saw something promising in Eric. He hired him in September 1955.

Eric had certainly faced rejection and had to make difficult decisions on his way to becoming a licensed and employed auto mechanic. But he persevered and he was rewarded for his perseverance. Each of Eric's employers, from Harold Robinson at Citadel Motors in 1944 to George

```
                                        27 Prescott  t.,
                                          Halifax, N.S.
                                          21 Sept,1954.
```

Dear Sir:
          I here by wish to apply for the job as mechanic in
the City Field Garage.
          I have held my mechanics license  since 1948.  From
1950 to 1952  I lived in Ontario at which time  I worked
and held my license in that province.  The following years
I have lived in the city of Halifax and have my license for
this province.
          I am a married man with one child.
             Hoping you will give this application favorable
consideration.   I remain,

```
                                 Yours very truly,
```

                                 Eric Davidson.

Letter that Eric sent to the City of Halifax seeking employment in 1954. Mary typed the letter and Eric signed it.

West at the City of Halifax in 1955, recognized something exceptional in Eric and each of them gave him the opportunity to prove himself. These men had pioneering attitudes with regard to handicapped employees and none of them regretted their decision to employ Eric Davidson.

Eric was extremely happy. He had secured a permanent position working on Halifax city's fleet of vehicles, which included cars, trucks, and heavy equipment such as tandem trucks, garbage trucks, and street sweepers. With a small family to support, Eric had landed a job where he was receiving a regular salary with benefits and a pension. The security and comfort that this job offered him was enormous. He had proven to himself and everyone that he could achieve whatever he set his mind to. He had reached the pinnacle of his career.

Eric made lifetime friends working at City Field and one of those friends was Pat Noddin, who was, when I spoke to him in 2017, eighty-seven years old. Pat remembers Eric working on all of the City equipment and that nothing could fool him. He recalls that Eric even replaced tracks on the winter Bombadiers. Pat's most vivid recollection is of Eric working on a carburetor. Eric would set a cloth down on his workbench and place all of the carburetor parts onto the cloth. He would then examine each part, pinching tiny springs with his fingers to gauge tension and rolling steel balls between his fingers to remember each one's size and where each belonged in the carburetor.

Pat fondly recalled a visit Eric made to his family home one Christmas when one of his sons received a toy fire engine as a gift. The youngster took the fire engine to Eric and laid it on his lap. Eric ran his hand over the toy and explained each part of the truck to the child. Pat said that he will always remember how Eric's hands moved back and forth over the toy.

Pat was fleet superintendent when the National Film Board came to City Field to film their documentary about Eric Davidson, *Just One of the Boys.* Pat also accompanied Eric to a city council meeting at Halifax City Hall where the film was screened for council in 1976. After council had viewed the film, the councillors lined up to shake Eric's hand. Pat said Eric was uncomfortable with the fuss and was glad when it was over.

Just one of the boys is a good descriptive of my father's view of himself. The boys were his brothers—the boys at work, the boys from the antique car club he later belonged to, the boys from his school days, and so on. The documentary is a poignant and inspirational fifteen-minute film, which superbly captures the essence of my father.

When the documentary shows Eric at work at City Field, he is wearing his grease-stained coveralls. In one scene, Allan Curran appears and asks Eric how he is getting on. He gives him a work order to put a new fuel pump on a vehicle. Eric tells the interviewer the work could be dangerous if he did not know all of the engine parts and if he didn't know exactly what he was working with. "Anyone can do it…anyone in my condition can do exactly what I am doing," he says with conviction.

In another segment of the documentary, my father explains to the interviewer that he was two years old when he lost his sight. "I was standing at the window looking out to see these ships on fire…there was pretty near two thousand people killed, so I was one of the lucky ones."

Eric also speaks about always being interested in automobile mechanics: "Even when I was in school, I would get these little manuals, and I'd get someone to read them to me. I got to know the principle of the engine and the way the car worked." He tells the documentary crew that his parents knew he wanted to work on car engines and they told him, "Go ahead if you think you can," while others were skeptical, telling him not to expect success.

Another City employee, Lot Cossar, was a building inspector when he first met Eric in the mid-1960s, a full decade before the documentary was made. He knew Eric as the blind mechanic. He also recognized him from seeing him walking in the North End because Lot lived in the same neighbourhood as Eric.

Lot recalled one day when Eric arrived at City Hall with another employee. At the time, Lot was having problems with his 1966 Ford Mustang and the Ford dealership was not able to remedy the problem. Someone suggested to Lot that he drive Eric back to City Field in the Mustang and let Eric diagnose the problem. They drove around the city down to Point Pleasant Park and then to City Field.

As Eric exited the car, he laughed and told Lot that he knew what the problem was as soon as Lot had started the car, but he enjoyed the drive around town just the same. He told Lot that he needed a new water pump and to take the car back to the dealership and tell them to install one. Lot was floored that Eric could diagnose the problem simply by listening to the engine running but he did as Eric told him. The dealership installed the new water pump and the car ran like a charm. When Lot told the service manager at the dealership that City Field had a blind mechanic and that it was this blind mechanic who told him to replace the water pump, the service manager was dumbstruck.

On another occasion, Lot was driving a Mercury Cougar when he picked up Eric. As soon as they pulled away, Eric told Lot that his transmission was slipping. Sure enough, a few days later, the transmission was seized. Lot jokingly told Eric later that he didn't think he could afford to drive Eric around anymore because every time he did it cost him money for car repairs.

On visits to City Field, Lot marvelled at Eric working on the various pieces of city equipment. He recalled one such visit when Eric had a Bombardier CJ7 snow machine complete with rubber tracks laid out on the floor disassembled. These machines were used by the City to remove snow, mostly from city sidewalks. Eric knew where every part was and where it belonged on the machine. Lot had much respect for Eric and his knowledge of automobiles.

When Lot happened upon a barn full of antique cars and car parts in Sackville, he knew right away he must contact Eric because he knew that Eric's hobby was antique cars. When Eric arrived at the barn, he examined the cars and each of the car parts, feeling the headlights and fenders with his hands. Eric identified the make and style of the car correctly every time and he did the same with each of the individual car parts. Lot was totally amazed at Eric's ability to identify a car or a car part simply by running his hands over them.

Eric enjoyed working at City Field, and he rarely missed a day of work in the twenty-five years he worked there. The City Field garage was originally located on Bell Road in Halifax which was an easy commute to and from work on the bus for Eric. He enjoyed this location because he could stroll in the Public Gardens at lunchtime and take pleasure in the peacefulness there.

Eric and co-workers at Halifax City Field in 1980. Pat Noddin, his supervisor and good friend, is standing at the far left, middle row. Eric is second from the right in the middle row.

When City Field relocated to a site off of Lady Hammond Road in the city's North End, Eric's co-workers insisted on driving him to and from work.

Occasionally some co-workers would pull pranks on Eric by taking some of his carefully placed tools out of his toolbox and putting them where he could not find them. These men did not necessarily mean to be cruel but their actions were belittling. Eric would simply say, "Okay boys, put it back." This was just one of the things Eric occasionally had to deal with to fit into the sighted world and he handled it well. He was well liked and highly respected by his peers and his employers.

In 1980, at sixty-five, Eric retired from City Field.

# Raising a Family

[B]eing blind is just one more thing to deal with. Day to day decisions have to be made and as a father values have to be passed on to children and beliefs and goals strived for. [11]

My father was thrilled to be a father, and as each of his babies was born he was filled with pride. My brother John was born in 1951 and I was born in 1955, just a few months before Dad became employed with City Field. Andrew was born in 1959.

A close family friend recalled that when my parents brought me home from the hospital, Dad said, "Isn't she a beautiful baby?" The friend was touched that my father spoke as though he could actually see me. She found it odd that my father used the word "see" or "look" in everyday conversation even though he was blind. He did see, just not with his eyes. To see what we looked like Dad gently felt our heads and tenderly ran his hands over our faces. He marvelled at our tiny fingers and toes. The beauty of an infant can be discerned by touch as well as by sight and our tiny features were beautiful to him. Dad would brush his lips across our heads planting little kisses and murmur endearments to us.

---

11 Eric Davidson quote in Kelly, "Public Becoming more Aware of and Helpful to Blind People."

Grandmother Georgina looking over Eric's shoulder while Mary holds baby John in Toronto, September 1951.

Sounds were another way for Dad to see. He delighted at listening to our murmurs and humming sounds as we nursed, our soft breathing as we slept, and our first attempts at giggling and speaking. As we became toddlers and youngsters, he often stopped what he was doing so that he could listen to us at play as we ran through the house or the neighbourhood screaming and hollering and he would laugh heartily as we ran by him. He watched us at play by listening to us at play.

My father was not a tall man. He stood about five foot seven, his frame lithe, more resembling the Davidson line than the Williams line. His face was kind and gentle and he smiled more than he frowned because he was a cheery sort. There were many scars on his face and around his eyes from injuries he sustained when the window exploded in upon him in the Halifax Explosion. Most notably there was a scar on his left eyebrow and a long scar that ran from under his left nostril down across his lips to his chin and another smaller scar below his right cheek. None of these scars had a negative effect on his appearance and I actually thought they made him look quite handsome and rugged. His hair was thinning too when we were young and he used to say that my brothers and I pulled his hair out when we were babies.

My father's hands were strong and beautiful to me. As a little girl, I liked to hold his hands palm up and marvel at the lines and callouses. I asked him why his hands were so rough and dirty and he explained to me that his work with oily, greasy cars and trucks left his hands in hard shape. His fingernails were always short and neatly clipped but tarnished with grease and grime around the cuticles and under the nails. His fingers were cracked and rough to the touch and had grit wedged into the cracks and crevices. No matter how vigorously he washed his hands, and he was a bit of a clean freak, he could not remove all the signs of his trade. Yet his hands were gentle when he patted my head or as he held my hand.

When my father retired in 1980, his hands slowly returned to normal. Although he still tinkered with his restoration projects, the grease and the grime eventually disappeared and the rough calloused hands became soft. Rough and calloused or soft and smooth, my father's hands were a masterpiece to me, a work of art created from years of labouring on motor vehicle engines.

In the summer of 1958, my parents sold 27 Prescott Street and bought a three-bedroom two-storey house at 109 Cabot Street just a few blocks north. Although I was only three years old the day that we moved, I remember leaving the old house and walking north on Prescott Street holding my mother's hand. My father was at work and my brother John was in Mahone Bay at our maternal grandparents' home. It was a warm day and as Mom and I walked north on Prescott Street, the moving van slowly chugged along beside us. Our new house was on the north side of Cabot Street between Robie Street and Prescott Street and it was one of five identical houses on the block.

My parents were a bit sad to leave their first home for they had many happy memories attached to it. But the new house had more living space and it was very close to the new Mulgrave Park Elementary School at the corner of Sebastian and Robie Streets. Living close to the school was of paramount importance to my parents because they didn't want us to cross too many streets on our way to and from school. As well, the new house was heated by an oil furnace whereas the house on Prescott Street was heated by coal.

During the winter months at the old house, Dad had to take the cinders from the furnace and then load coal into the furnace each night before going to bed. The only thing the new house lacked was a garage so Dad rented a garage one block away on the Duffus Street Extension, which is now Wells Street. The street was renamed for Billy Wells, the firefighter who was driving the fire truck Patricia at the time of the Halifax Explosion.

The next year Andrew was born, and I remember standing on the doorstep watching my parents get into a taxi, leaving John and me at home with my mother's dear friend Dorothy O'Brien to look after us. I was only four years old at the time, so I didn't know why or where they were going but I certainly remember Mom and Dad coming home with a tiny baby boy. I thought he was wonderful, like a little doll. Andrew was a frail fellow though because he was born with asthma and he suffered frequent attacks as a baby. In those days when he had a severe asthma attack, Mom and Dad took him by taxi to the Children's Hospital, as it was known then, where he was put into an oxygen tent until he recovered. Sometimes my parents

Eric and Mary pose in their Cabot Street home for a photo in 1959 with their children, Marilyn (four), John (eight), and baby Andrew. Marilyn is happy to be sitting on her father's lap.

stayed overnight with Andrew. When this happened, Dorothy came to look after John and me. As well as the many trips to the hospital with Andrew, Mom and Dad spent many a sleepless night sitting up with him when he was having trouble breathing. For the first years of his life, Andrew rarely slept without the vaporizer operating in his bedroom. Mom and Dad were ever vigilant with him and they worried a great deal about Andrew in those early years. Fortunately he outgrew his childhood asthma.

Dad had nicknames for each of us children. I had two nicknames, Punkin Head or Sweetie Pie, and John's nickname was Weeshie. Andrew's nickname was Baba because that was the first word Andrew ever said. I vividly recall that evening after supper when Dad was talking baby talk to Andrew who was babbling away in his playpen in the living room. Dad cheered and said, "He said 'Baba'! He said 'Baba'!" and that is what Dad called Andrew from then on. My nicknames and John's nickname wore off as we grew older but Dad always called Andrew Baba, which was shortened to Ba when he got a little older.

Mom was a stay-at-home mom, a luxury by today's standards but quite common in the 1950s and 1960s when I grew up. In our home, Mom looked after us during the day but after supper our father took over and it was his time with us. Dad was very active in our lives, especially in our formative years, and he was a very involved father at a time when it wasn't common. It was crucial to Dad that he spend a good deal of time with us as he knew other visually impaired fathers whose children were strange with them because of their visual impairment.

Each night, he got us ready for bed making sure that we washed our hands and faces and brushed our teeth. Saturdays were bath nights and Dad supervised the baths too. He washed our hair and ensured that all the soap was rinsed out by pouring pitchers of water over our heads and feeling our hair until it was squeaky clean. He never left us unattended in the bathtub. Dad made sure that we said our prayers before we jumped into bed.

We said the children's prayer, "Now I Lay Me Down to Sleep," although Dad was not particularly fond of that prayer because of the sentence, "if I should die before I wake I pray the Lord my soul to take." He felt that line was morose. Then Dad told us a bedtime story. He either made up a story or he told us traditional stories such as "Little Red Riding Hood" or "Goldilocks and the Three Bears." Dad's invented stories were pirate stories for my brothers and stories about cats or bears for me. Most nights though, he fell asleep right in the midst of the story and we had to wake him up to finish. "Where did I leave off?" he'd say and then he picked up the story and carried on until either he fell asleep again or we fell asleep. Some nights he was just so tired that he fell asleep several times while telling the story. When he kissed us goodnight, he kissed the tops of our heads and murmured, "kiss a head" in endearment.

When I was not quite five, my father carried me outside onto the back veranda and introduced me to the night sky. I wasn't usually awake when it was dark out but that night Andrew was fussing with his asthma and Mom was tending to him. I got out of bed so Dad carried me outside and told me to gaze up at all the stars in the sky. I remember being fascinated by the celestial display because I had never seen the stars before. Although Dad could not see the stars, he knew that the night sky was full of them and more importantly he knew I could see them and that I would be captivated. He asked me to tell him what I saw up in the sky. I told him I saw lots of little lights. I was too young to know that my father could not see what I was seeing, but I was old enough to know that this was a special time for me with my father.

Another nighttime recollection was more of a frightening experience for me. I had been asleep in my bedroom and I woke up to hear a mouse near my dresser. I could hear it chewing on something. I was terrified of mice as a little girl and I still don't like them. I was frozen in fear and then I imagined that the mouse somehow jumped onto my bed.

I flew out of bed and hightailed it to my parents' bedroom. I must have given them each an awful fright when I jumped onto their bed screaming about a mouse. I snuggled up to Mom, terrified to return to my bed. Poor Dad got ousted from his bed and had to sleep in mine that night. The next day there was a mousetrap set in the room under the dresser. I never saw or heard the mouse again so the trap must have been effective. Dad wasn't fussy about handling traps and rodents but he had to do it occasionally and he would have ensured that his hands were gloved. My Dad the exterminator. I thought he was so brave. I felt safe.

Not long after the mouse episode I went to bed with bubble gum in my mouth. Dad came to give me my nightly kiss on the head and found my hair full of bubble gum. What a mess! I remember Dad chuckling and saying repeatedly, "poor Sweetie Pie" as he used his sense of touch and the scissors to snip the gummy mess out. I was not the least bit concerned that Dad would make a mess of my hair. He got me out of that sticky situation and he did a pretty good job too because I don't recall being teased about my hair afterwards.

A fond memory of my father that my brothers and I share equally is our fascination with Dad's gold pocket watch. His mother had given it to him on his eighteenth birthday and it was very precious to him. When he got dressed up in his best suit for church or other such occasions, he carried his pocket watch with him. It was a wonderful piece of jewellery and we were attracted to it like magpies. He always allowed us to examine the watch and he would patiently show us how he told the time by running his fingers over the Braille numerals. Although there were print numerals on the face, we liked to run our fingers over the Braille numerals just as Dad did. In a 1958 *Family Herald* magazine article about our father, John and I are pictured with Dad examining the gold pocket watch. John now has the cherished heirloom.

I looked forward to my father coming home from work each day. I would run to the bus stop at the top of Cabot Street to meet him. When he stepped off the bus, I shouted to him to let him know that I was there and I ran to his side. He would then fold up his white cane and tuck it into his coat pocket and we would walk home together hand in hand. He was always cheerful, never cranky or irritable, when he arrived home and he was genuinely happy when I met him at the bus stop. Once at home, he sat on the landing step inside the door to take off his work boots. All the while, I was hovering over him and clinging to his neck. I told him about whatever I had done that day and sometimes I sang him a new song that I had learned at school. A great favourite of ours was the Halloween song, "Who, oo, oo, oo, oo said the Owl, who's afraid of Halloween?"

Dad was always keen for me to sing my little songs for him and he never once told me that he was too busy to listen. One song that Dad enjoyed us singing together the most was Claude King's 1962 hit "Wolverton Mountain." The song is about Clifton Clowers who lives on a mountain and has a daughter that he keeps a watchful eye on. Dad used to say that he would be just like Clifton Clowers if any boys tried to woo me. It was a little joke between the two of us for years.

Another special thing between Dad and me was that whenever I baked a little cake in my Easy-Bake Oven, which was a popular toy in the 1960s, I always saved it for Dad, and when he got home from work he'd gobble it down, telling me how yummy it was and what a great baker I was.

As a little girl, I also liked to show Dad how tall I was growing or how long my hair was getting. He placed his hands on my head and ran them down the length of my hair to see for himself, and if I had a ponytail I shook it back and forth across his hands, which made him laugh. Quite often, I would pester him to show me his biceps or big muscles as I called them. He'd bend his arm and flex his muscles to humour me. To me he was the strongest man in the world.

While I knew my father could not see, I made birthday cards and Father's Day cards for him just as any little girl would do and I read them to him and described what I had drawn on the card, which was usually an antique automobile. He was always genuinely happy to receive them and he ran his fingers over my drawings and lettering. My father saved the cards and now they are more special to me than when I originally made them.

Whenever we got sick as children and regardless of who was sick, whether it was Andrew, John, or me, Dad would be visibly upset and fretting. The first thing he would do upon arriving home from work was to check on the sick patient. When we were feeling better, he was much relieved.

My mother suffered from horrific migraine headaches every month as a young woman. She would be in bed retching on and off, sometimes for two days. Dad was always attentive to Mom but especially so when she was sick. He would tenderly hold her hair off of her face as she retched into a basin. He would then empty the basin into the toilet and rinse it out. He placed cooling cloths on my mother's forehead. At these times, the house was quiet, no noisy playing. On a few occasions Mom was so sick that Dad called the doctor to make a house call and relieve her suffering with an injection of medication. My brothers and I learned at a fairly young age how to take care of ourselves while Mom was sick and Dad was at work. At about seven or eight years old, I began caring for my mother when she was down with a migraine and Dad was at work. I didn't mind it, with the exception of emptying the basin and rinsing it out. Mom missed out on a lot of family outings because of the migraine headaches but miraculously when she reached her fifties they disappeared and she was able to enjoy her life so much more.

Dad's compassion did not end with our immediate family. Dad was a frequent visitor to local hospitals and nursing homes when any of his friends, co-workers, or other family members were hospitalized. I often accompanied my father, and whomever we were visiting was always happy to see Dad. He visited the old Victoria General Hospital so often that the nurses and custodians knew him by name.

While both of my parents were legally blind, anyone observing our everyday life would see little difference between our family and the families of sighted parents in our working-class neighbourhood of North End Halifax. We had birthday parties, picnics, summer trips outside the city, and our everyday life was very similar to theirs.

Mom looked after us children, managed the household, and prepared meals like the other neighbourhood women. Dad went off to work each day carrying his metal lunchbox like the other men except he walked to the bus with his white cane. Dad shovelled snow in the winter and he mowed the grass with a push mower in the summer. Our property never showed signs of neglect and looked just as cheery and as well maintained as the other houses on the street. Dad was quite capable of doing most of the maintenance, such as replacing storm windows. He had each of the storm windows marked for the corresponding windows they went onto so there was never a mix-up.

Physically marking property was a common practice for my father because it was a sure way to identify his property when people occasionally tried to take advantage of his disability. He marked our trikes and bikes, his lawnmower, and tools to name a few. John recalls that his sled was stolen one winter when we lived at 27 Prescott Street. He spotted it sitting in a neighbourhood yard and reported this to Dad, who then approached the neighbour about the sled in the yard. The neighbour insisted that it belonged to his children. Unbeknownst to the neighbour, Dad had marked one of the runners with a file. Dad could feel with his hands things that a sighted person could barely see, so when Dad directed the neighbour's attention to the marked runner the neighbour was speechless. Dad had him dead to rights and the sled was returned.

When Dad built something, he was particular about detail. Shortly after moving into the Cabot Street house, Dad tore down the front and back entrance steps because they were rotted and weak. He then built the two new sets of steps and verandas on his own. The next-door neighbour was impressed as he watched Dad working with hammer, nails, and his Brailled level. Dad's forms for the concrete were straight and the concrete was poured so all posts were even and level. The deck was secured to the foundation with lag bolts and the floor planking was level. The newel posts and railings were straight and solid and the steps were perfect too. Dad was a hard act to follow. The neighbour could not compete with Dad so he hired someone to build his veranda.

Dad had learned how to handle carpentry tools when he was a student at the School for the Blind. He did not tentatively tap on the nail. Instead he took full swings and hit the nail square and he rarely hit his fingers with the hammer. He held the nail with his thumb and index finger while the other three fingers of that hand were used to position the nail. He would lightly tap the nail to start it and then increase the force with each swing until the nail was fully driven into place. Between strikes, Dad's fingers closed on the nail and opened just before the hammer struck. He hammered at the same pace as a sighted person so his fingers were opening and closing very quickly. Occasionally Dad got a wood or metal splinter in his fingers and he would ask one of us children to remove it with the tweezers. Whenever I removed a splinter for Dad, he did not wince and I thought he was so brave. Dad built John a beautiful buggy with big strong wheels for soapbox racing and John won a lot of races with it. He built a soapbox racer for Andrew too. John still has a little truck that Dad built for him.

When my parents laid the attic floor on Cabot Street, John was tasked to help. Mom stood on the back veranda and handed the boards up to Dad, who was standing on the porch roof above the side door of the house. Dad then handed the boards to John through the open attic window. When all the boards were inside, Dad laid them down and just like that John and I had a playroom. Attics also served as storerooms and our attic was no different. Mom stored many things up there and one of those things was her wedding cake. In those days it was a common practice and considered good luck to save some of your wedding cake. One day while John and I were playing in the attic, we decided to do a little rummaging and lo and behold we found a healthy supply of cake with tiny silver candies in the icing. Without asking Mom's permission, we feasted on the cake. We returned to the scene of the crime several times before we got caught. We weren't punished but what was left of the cake was thrown away.

The neighbourhood demographic was mostly young families so there were always children to play with. Winter or summer we played outside.

Our house backed on the city reservoir, which provided us children with an ideal hill for tobogganing in the winter. There wasn't a fence around it then as there is now. We would often toboggan and play outside until our fingers and toes were nearly frozen. We'd come inside and howl in agony as our fingers slowly warmed up. Mom would admonish us for not having the good sense to come in before we got to that stage. I have memories of standing with my toes tucked under the radiator and my hands on top of the radiator in an effort to warm them up quicker. In the summer, we were permitted to play outside until the street lights came on which was pretty much the rule for all of the neighbourhood children. Some summer evenings Mom had to coax us into the house if we ignored the street-light rule. By coax I mean that once Mom appeared we scattered and ran home because she was carrying a fly swatter tucked behind her back and we were the intended flies. She never had to use the swatter on us but it was a very effective scare tactic.

We may have been one of the first families in the neighbourhood to get a black-and-white TV!  It was 1962 and I was seven. John and I were beside ourselves with excitement and we couldn't get enough TV initially. Cartoons were aired on Saturday mornings but Sunday was the best because the Walt Disney show aired on Sunday evenings. Our neighbourhood friends often joined us to watch TV too. Mom and Dad watched *Don Messer's Jubilee* and weatherman Rube Hornstein on CBC. Shortly after we got the TV, I watched my first Shirley Temple movie, *The Little Princess*. The movie is about a little girl who searches military hospitals after the First World War looking for her father, and like all Shirley Temple movies it was a tear-jerker. I cried quite a bit and Dad felt so bad for me. "Poor Sweetie Pie," he said over and over. He couldn't bear to hear me cry so he took me to a hardware store on Agricola Street and bought me a doll. Dad knew a doll would make me feel better. He was right.

In the summers it was routine for Dad to take us to Tootsies for an ice cream cone or some candy treats in the early evening after supper. Tootsies was the little store on the corner of Agricola and Merkel Streets only a few blocks from our house. If I was playing outside with my friends, Dad would invite them to come along and he always bought a treat for them too. He looked like the Pied Piper heading down the street with me holding his hand and a string of children following close behind. Needless to say all the neighbourhood kids liked my father. We often brought Mom home a vanilla ice cream cone too and it was covered with tissue paper to protect it.

Being a redhead, I was teased about my red hair when I was a child. I remember the first time. I was in grade primary and on my way home from school one day. The kids said that my father must be the milkman because my hair was red. When I told Mom, she laughed and told me that the milkman was not my father and that my red hair was special and that I was special and because of that the kids were jealous of me.

But I was subjected to ridicule and I was even attacked because of my parents' physical handicaps. Once, some children who lived for a brief time in our neighbourhood tormented me, saying that because my parents were blind I would be blind one day too. I was quite scrappy as a child, so I gave back as good as I got.

The worst incident though was when I was invited by a classmate to play with her and three of her friends whom I did not know. There were also several women having tea in the living room so we girls went to a bedroom to play. Without warning, I was pushed to the floor and held down by a few of the girls while another girl tried to pour something into my eyes. My classmate just stood by and watched. I didn't know what they were trying to pour into my eyes, but they were laughing and saying that they were going to make me blind like my father. I fought like a wild animal and managed to escape, running from the bedroom to the living room. I screamed at the women and told them what had just happened to me. Then I ran home. I could not believe that these women did not hear me screaming in the bedroom and did not come to see what was going on. I never told Mom or Dad about this incident because I thought it would upset them and because I felt stupid that I had been so duped. I never spoke to that girl again.

# Vacations

Like most families in the neighbourhood, we did not own a modern car for everyday driving. We walked or we used public transit or a taxi for transportation. Public transit in those days was trolley buses, which were electric buses that drew power from overhead wires using spring-loaded trolley poles. The drivers knew my father's name and Dad knew their names too because he was such a frequent rider. They'd greet Dad as he entered the bus and Dad always spoke their name in response upon hearing their voice.

Dad sat in the first seat opposite the bus driver and he and the driver would chat back and forth about mutual interests for the entire ride. Riding on the buses was much different back in the 1960s and 1970s than it is today. Drivers were permitted to chat with riders. The drivers knew that Dad was blinded in the Halifax Explosion and it was obvious that they admired him.

Quite often, passengers on the trolley knew Dad and they would come sit by us and chat with him or simply greet him. On occasion though, while riding on the trolley buses, people would stare at my father. When this happened, I glared back until they looked away. It hurt me when people looked at my father that way and I still find it impolite when people stare at someone who is different in appearance. Dad travelled by bus throughout Halifax until he was in his late eighties and his health forced him to stop.

Marjorie (three) and Eric (one) in the summer of 1916.

Braille love letter sent by Eric to Mary when he was working in Ottawa a few months before their marriage. Eric had a friend address the letter to Mary for him.

Mary and Eric cutting their wedding cake, Ottawa, August 1950. Marilyn and John enjoyed some of this cake years later.

Eric using a feeler gauge as he completes a valve job
on a truck at Patterson Motors in Ottawa, 1950.

Mary knit Christmas stockings for her children,
grandchildren, and many others. She won first prize
several times for her knitted items at the Canadian
National Exhibition in Toronto.

Reed-worked chair made by Eric while he attended the Halifax School for the Blind.

Eric and Mary with Marilyn, John (standing centre), and Andrew, 1998.

Eric strumming his banjo on his fiftieth wedding anniversary, August 2000, Kane Street.

Eric with his granddaughter Andrea in 1979.

The Memorial Bell Tower at Fort Needham on the day of the one-hundredth-anniversary memorial service on December 6, 2017.

A pin on the author's coat during the one-hundredth-anniversary memorial service on December 6, 2017, a wet and blustery day.

In the 1960s, I took piano lessons on Church Street located off of Morris Street in the South End. My teacher was May Baker and she was a very good friend of my mother. May was visually impaired and an excellent teacher and pianist. At the end of my lesson, Dad and I would meet at the bus stop on the corner of Spring Garden Road and Queen Street right in front of the Royal Bank. Dad walked from City Field on Bell Road to meet me and he was always there waiting for me. I'd say, "I'm here Dad," and grab his hand and we went home together. Each year there was a piano recital in June and Dad always recorded mine.

Our first trip away together was in the summer of 1957 when Mom and Dad took John and me to Rhode Island in the United States to visit our great aunts. While we were boarding the train on the return trip home, a woman became incensed and told Dad that he was carrying me like a turkey under his arm and not like a child should be carried. Mom and Dad often chuckled about that in later years. Of course, Dad had a very good hold of me and I was in no danger.

We regularly visited our Zinck grandparents in Mahone Bay, which is a picturesque seaside village located roughly fifty miles from Halifax on the South Shore. We travelled back and forth on the old Acadian Lines buses. My grandfather worked in nearby Lunenburg as a shipbuilder and the most notable ship he worked on was the replica of the *Bounty* built in 1960. Our grandparents' home was on Church Street around the corner from the famous three churches and practically a stone's throw to the bay. In the mornings, awakening to the sound of the seagulls in the bay was enchanting. Nanny and Grampy had a lovely vegetable garden and a flower garden, and fresh flowers from Nanny's garden were ever present on the kitchen table, filling the room with sweet aromas. John and I thought it was a great treat to pick ripe tomatoes from the garden and eat them like apples. The kitchen was a huge country kitchen with an old-fashioned wood stove and a rocking chair nearby. It was so cozy.

We looked forward to these visits because the house was much bigger than ours and it was great for hide-and-seek games. On one of these visits when I was about five years old, John coaxed me to jump over something on the ground and when I did I jumped right into a wasp nest. I got my feet stung repeatedly. Mom heard the commotion. She carried me into the kitchen and sat with me on her lap, rocking me back and forth and kissing my feet. Mom didn't fuss over us when we scraped our knees or otherwise hurt ourselves. She usually examined the injury, cleaned it, and said, "you'll live," before sending us off to continue playing, so when I got that much attention from my mother I lapped it up like a kitten.

The first family vacation that we took with our complete family of five was in the summer of 1960 when Andrew was only a baby. Mom and Dad rented a rustic cottage in the South Shore community of Blandford for a week. This was my first introduction to an outhouse and I did not like it. The spiders and the smell terrified me, so either Mom or Dad would have to stand outside offering moral support when I visited the outhouse. They indulged me for sure and I have always been most appreciative.

We were right across the road from the beach and we went swimming almost every day. Dad supervised our swimming while Mom relaxed with little Andrew back at the cottage. Dad enjoyed sitting on the beach, soaking up the sun, just listening to us splashing and carrying on. As luck would have it, there was a convenience store near the beach and Dad treated us to ice cream cones after our day at the beach. In the evenings, we played a lot of checkers and board games.

While we were there, I met a girl who lived across the road and we played together. I was even invited to stay for supper. John and I had our first horse ride there too. I don't recall how we managed to get the ride but I do remember both of us sitting on the horse together and I felt like I was going to fall off as the horse sauntered along the road led by its owner. It was on this horse that I spotted a two-dollar bill lying in the ditch and once the ride was over I scooted back to the ditch and gleefully retrieved the bill. When we returned to the city, Mom took me to the bank and we opened my first bank account with the two-dollar deposit.

The next family trip was in 1962. I'm sure we must have turned a few heads as we travelled—two visually impaired parents with three young children and toting suitcases. We travelled as usual on the Acadian Lines bus, this time to Berwick where we stayed for a week at the United Church camp there. Berwick is a charming town situated west of Halifax in the breathtaking Annapolis Valley. The church camp was a wonderful experience for our entire family with each day full of fun activities for the children and a variety of activities for the adults too. I did not like the nights though because our little cottage had ants. Dad as ever understood my fear and he stayed with me each night until I nodded off to sleep. Mom and Dad really enjoyed this restful and reflective week at the church camp and they made several lifelong friends. Little did we know then that Dad and Mom would spend the last years of their lives directly across the street from the church camp.

Trains were Dad's preferred method of travel because they were relaxing and he enjoyed the rocking of the railcar and the clickety-clack of the wheels on the tracks. Dad could freely walk about the train and the porters usually permitted him to stand between the cars and smoke his pipe. There he could listen to the locomotive pulling up ahead. Occasionally, he was permitted to have the window open so that he could feel the wind on his face. Everything about travelling on the train was perfect for Dad.

In 1963, there was a coal locomotive train going on its last run from Joggins to Maccan and the public was invited to attend. Dad, John, and Dad's friend Ken Waterman drove to Joggins in Dad's 1934 Rolls Royce. They were invited to ride the entire excursion in the cab of the locomotive. Dad and John sat in the fireman's seat while the fireman shovelled coal into the firebox. Occasions like this when we were children made us realize that our father was someone special as no one else was invited to ride in the cab. Dad enjoyed the myriad of sounds inside and outside the cab as well as the smells of the coal, the grease, and the steam. He had his trusty tape recorder with him and he recorded the entire trip. Listening to that recording I can hear in Dad's voice his keen interest in the entire operation as he chats with the engineer.

Because of Mom's fond memories of life on the farm as a child, she wanted us children to experience farm life too. So in 1964, she put an advertisement in the local newspaper looking for a working farm in Lunenburg County that would board a family of five for a week. Her ad was answered by the Rafuse family who had a farm in the small inland community of Parkdale. The farm consisted of a sprawling farmhouse with three barns, one each for the cattle, pigs, and poultry. Off we went for a week in the country and it was a fantastic vacation.

We had wagon rides, we watched the men haying, and the milking operations in the big barn, we gathered eggs, fed the pigs, and dined on country-style meals with fresh homemade bread each day. I tasted homemade baked beans for the first time that summer and they were delicious. We swam at the lake, which was only a short walk through the woods. The Parkdale Maplewood Field Day, which included ox pulls, games of chance, baked goods, and so much more, was a first for us too. We were city slickers getting a glimpse of farm life and enjoying country living to the fullest. We ran so much each day that we simply collapsed in bed each night.

One day, Dad, John and I went with the men to haul logs out of the woods. We rode on the back of the empty wagon that was hauled by a tractor. Once the wagon was loaded with logs, we crawled back onto the wagon, this time on top of the logs. All was fine until I decided to show off and stand up on the logs. The wagon lurched to one side, and off onto the ground I flew right into the tire ruts, with the rear wheels coming toward me. John yelled for me to roll and I rolled until the tractor and wagon finally stopped. I can imagine the fear and feeling of helplessness that must have gripped my poor father when all this was happening but he did not reprimand me for my carelessness because he was so happy I was unhurt.

Mr. Rafuse took Dad, John, and me in the complete night darkness to nearby Whetstone Lake one evening so Dad could record the frogs. There were so many constellations in the sky that I was mesmerized by it all. The night sky in the country offered tenfold the stars that I had seen in the city. I also saw a real firefly for the first time in my life and the darkness was alight with them. It was a special night there listening to the frogs with Dad and John, watching fireflies and staring at the magnificent night sky. The following two summers John and I returned to the Parkdale farm because we enjoyed ourselves so much there, and Mom and Dad were only too happy to oblige us. I'm sure the two weeks that John and I were away offered a bit of a break for our parents as well.

By 1971, our family vacations had come to an end as John and I were working during the summers. We did take day trips, mostly to the South Shore to visit Mom's relatives, and to the Annapolis Valley.

# Shopping with Dad

Dad's prostheses fit him so perfectly that often people unfamiliar with him did not even know that he was without sight. He wore clear eyeglasses when he got dressed up, which made him look quite polished, but otherwise he went without eyeglasses. He did not wear glasses to work or when he worked on automobiles in his garage either.

Dad was always very guarded and private about his ocular prostheses. He removed and cleaned them every night and he carefully stored them in his dresser, but I never saw him remove or adjust them at any time when I was a child. He kept this part of his life away from us when we were children because he did not want us to be frightened of him.

Over the years Dad had his prosthetic eyes cleaned, reglazed, and replaced routinely as required. However, when Dad reached his seventies his prostheses did not fit quite as well due to muscular atrophy. Occasionally, one of his artificial eyes would fall out or we would have to tell Dad that an eye adjustment was necessary, which was very humiliating for him. Because of the muscular atrophy, it was also easy for dust and dirt to get into Dad's eye sockets. Skin grafts were the only way to prevent the eyes from falling out and that operation was not desirable at his age.

So in 1996, he was prescribed his first pair of dark eyeglasses, which to a degree helped prevent his eyes from falling out and also prevented dirt from

Eric looking very polished, 1950. His glass eyes looked so real that people unfamiliar with him did not realize he was blind.

getting into his eye sockets. The dark glasses masked his eyes, which had a habit of moving about in his eye sockets. Dad was very conscious of his appearance and he wanted to avoid embarrassment for himself or discomfort for anyone else.

Sometimes, Dad asked me or my brothers to assist him with little things like finding misplaced items or choosing a tie to match his shirt and of course reading. And sometimes, he asked us to explain to him what various things looked like. He had no recollection of colour because he was too young when he lost his sight so it was not possible for us to describe colour.

If the item was something that he had not physically examined before, he could not visualize it, so whenever possible we took Dad to the object so he could feel it. Most of the time Dad was able to examine an object but if not, we described it by its shape, either round, square, rectangular, or triangular, and by its dimensions so he could gauge its size, large or small.

Although Dad would have qualified for a Seeing Eye dog, he felt a guide dog would give him no more independence than he already had and furthermore a dog was a huge responsibility.

When Dad travelled by himself, he always used his white cane to guide him. His cane was collapsible and easily folded up to fit in his coat pocket when he reached his destination. Dad navigated around obstacles almost as well as a sighted person. He always walked with his back straight and his head tilted slightly to one side, listening intently. He held his cane in front of him at about a forty-five-degree angle with a slight sweeping motion, frequently tapping the ground to check for obstacles. He was not timid when he walked by himself and he walked briskly because he had confidence in his ability. He liked to "charge" along as he said. This fooled a lot of people into thinking that Dad must have had some vision.

When I walked with Dad and someone was walking slowly in front of us, Dad would be anxious to pass by them. I still walk too quickly for most people and whenever I have to adjust to their speed I smile and think of my father and our many walks together.

Dad relied on sound much more than a sighted person and his hearing was extremely acute. Along with his white cane, Dad used sound to guide him. In a way he had his own built-in sonar navigation system. He used echolocation and listened for the sound of his footsteps bouncing off of the sidewalk curbs or other obstacles nearby to guide him safely as he walked along. When he crossed a street, he listened to the traffic flow before stepping from the safety of the sidewalk. When he judged it safe to cross, he proceeded and this system worked well for him long before audio crosswalks were introduced. Dad knew exactly when to step up onto the curb and he knew when he was approaching anything such as a wall or a structure because of the echoes his footsteps made. Dad memorized the number of steps in places he was familiar with. When I accompanied my father to buildings he was not familiar with, I counted the stairs and told him how many there were.

We learned very early that it was imperative that our toys were not left lying about the floor or on steps, creating hazards for our father. We did our best to be tidy and put things back where they belonged but we were children and sometimes we were careless. Fortunately, our carelessness never resulted in any serious falls, but there were some crushed toys.

Occasionally, something such as a tricycle left on the sidewalk could trip Dad up. Fortunately, he was as agile as a cat and whenever he bumped into anything or tripped over something, he corrected and carried on. However, it was embarrassing for him and if the mood struck him, the offending article was tossed or kicked aside. Such an incident occurred when he collided with an empty metal garbage can that had been left in the middle of the sidewalk as he went to work one morning. Dad lined the can up like a football and kicked it. There was likely a dandy dent in the side of the can when the owner retrieved it.

When I was a little girl, I always held my father's hand as we walked along but when I got older Dad hooked his arm through mine. Once my brothers and I proved ourselves capable to guide him, he would leave the white cane behind and trust us. I failed miserably on one of my earliest excursions downtown with my father. We were walking along Barrington Street one Saturday morning. Dad had his white cane with him and I was holding his hand. However, I wasn't watching where I was going and I smacked my head on something that was attached to a lamppost.

Dad knelt down and picked me up. I was crying. Dad comforted me and said "poor Sweetie Pie" as he swept his hand across my head to determine if I was bleeding from my injury. When he was satisfied that I was not and I had stopped crying, Dad set me down and we walked on to the CNIB canteen in the Roy Building and he bought me a small container of chocolate milk to further console me. Dad was genuinely upset that I had hurt myself and he was eager to make me feel better.

Saturday morning shopping expeditions with my father when I was a little girl were special times. Dad always put on his everyday suit and his fedora hat and off we went on the trolley bus downtown to Barrington Street and Spring Garden Road. These weekly excursions always included a visit to the CNIB canteen in the Roy Building. Of course, Dad knew the visually impaired gentleman operating the canteen. His name was Carroll Boehner and I remember him being quite tall, soft-spoken, and having a wonderful smile. Our visits were always chatty and quite often I got some chocolate milk. Sometimes, there were other visually impaired patrons visiting Mr. Boehner as well. It seemed to be a regular Saturday morning meeting place for Dad and his friends.

Our shopping trips usually included visits to the Eaton's and Zellers department stores, both located on the east side of Barrington Street with Eaton's cornering Prince Street and Zellers cornering Sackville Street. Eaton's was a grand store with three levels. Marble steps and a shiny brass handrail led from the main floor to the top floor. There was also an elevator operated by a man in uniform and hat. On the upper level was a bathroom, which required a dime to access the toilet. Zellers had three floors as well with an elegant staircase to the upper floor. The main attraction for me at Zellers was the soft-ice-cream machine on the main floor just inside the front doors.

Dad often visited the Sievert tobacco shop just south of Zellers on Barrington Street to replenish his tobacco supply or to buy a new pipe or pipe cleaners. At Phinney's, across the street from Eaton's, Dad bought strings for his banjo and occasionally some bluegrass records. While Dad often bought John a dinky toy on their downtown excursions, Dad bought me edible treats. On Spring Garden Road, we visited the Candy Bowl, the most wonderful store a child could experience. I will recall forever the sweet smell of chocolate and mint, and a myriad of other candy smells as we entered the store. My favourite treat was Smarties or chocolate blocks sold by the pound. Of course, Dad did not buy a pound! But Dad had a sweet tooth too, so another favourite stop for us downtown was The Cake Box, a bakery on Blowers Street. A family favourite was doughnuts fresh out of the fryer and still warm.

Saturdays following Family Allowance day each month usually meant shopping for new clothing, shoes, or other necessities. Family Allowance was a small financial award paid by the federal government for each child under sixteen years of age. Mom used the allowance for our clothing, shoes, and whatever else we needed. She took us shopping at the Metropolitan and Woolworths stores on Gottingen Street. If we didn't need anything some months, Mom deposited the money into each of our bank savings accounts.

Toys such as bicycles were purchased second-hand. I remember going with Dad to a house near the Halifax Forum to buy a used bike for me. The gentleman selling the bike was surprised when we arrived, as he was not expecting a blind man with a little girl in tow. Dad examined the bike completely with his hands, feeling for imperfections or anything out of the ordinary. The bike passed Dad's inspection and I rode it home to Cabot Street with Dad walking along beside me. Andrew was the only one to get a new bicycle for his birthday when he was a young lad. Dad took him to Calhoun's Bicycle Shop, which was located on the corner of Agricola Street and Cunard Street, and Andrew picked out the bike he wanted. It was red with a banana seat and high handlebars. We certainly kept Dad busy repairing our tire punctures and any chain damage on our bikes.

My most memorable Saturday morning trips downtown with Dad were each year in December. He took me and my brothers to see the magnificent Nova Scotia Light and Power Christmas display *Fantasyland* in the basement level of the Capitol Theatre building on Barrington Street at the foot of Spring Garden Road. This lighted and actively moving display with Santa and Mrs. Claus, Frosty the Snowman, and a myriad of nursery-rhyme and toy characters was a jaw-dropping experience for me and I looked forward to it each year. Even though I was a teenager when the NSL&P ceased *Fantasyland* in the early 1970s, I was saddened to see it disappear.

As I got older, Dad began to rely on me to help him shop for Mom for her birthday and for Christmas, and I soon accompanied Dad whenever he shopped for Mom, Marjorie, or his mother. What started as little weekly trips together downtown became a lifetime of shopping together. Dad's Saturday morning trips downtown remained the same for many years after we had grown up. He was travelling alone though and he only visited the Sievert tobacco shop and the Halifax Folklore Centre, as the Cake Box, Candy Bowl, Eaton's, Zellers, and Phinney's had all closed by then.

Whether my father went shopping alone or with us children, he was adept at handling cash. He knew each coin by its size and shape. For example, nickels had eight edges, pennies were completely round, dimes were smallest with a grooved edging, and so on. By feeling each coin, he knew what change he needed and he knew what change he received.

Long before tactile bills were introduced in 2001, Dad had a system for identifying his dollar bills. He carried his bills folded in half with the one-dollar bills on the outside. Next were the twos, fives, tens, and the twenty-dollar bills folded into the middle. He always knew how many of each denomination he was carrying before he left the house. If he was unsure, he would have Mom or one of us children check that for him. He kept a record in his mind of how much he spent and what denomination of bills he came home with.

# Family Life

Dad was an excellent skater and skating was a sport that he thoroughly enjoyed from the time he was a youngster. So in the winter, he often took us skating on Chocolate Lake, which is near the Armdale Rotary in Halifax, or to Papermill Lake, which is off the Hammonds Plains Road in Bedford. We only went skating when Dad knew for sure that the ice was frozen thick and solid. He found out ice conditions by asking his friends who were familiar with the lakes or by listening to ice-condition reports on the radio.

We skated at Papermill Lake more often than anywhere else. We travelled by the Acadia Lines bus to Bedford and walked up the Hammonds Plains Road to the lake. It was just a short walk. Dad laced up and tied my skates for me. When he had his skates on, he took my hand and we skated together around the lake. There was rarely anyone else skating when we were there so Dad would open up and skate freely without fear of bumping into anyone. He often took us to Papermill Lake in the summer to swim too.

Whether it was winter skating or summer swimming at Papermill, no trip with Dad would be complete without a treat. Conveniently, there was a corner store on the Bedford Highway at the bottom of the Plains Road where we waited for the bus back to Halifax, and Dad always bought us a treat for the bus ride home.

The Bill Lynch fairs on the Halifax Commons were always fun for me and my brothers. How excited we got when the fair came to town. Dad took us to the fair each summer when we were little ones and our favourite ride was the ferris wheel. Dad didn't care for amusement park rides so we rode alone. As we neared the bottom on each revolution of the ferris wheel, we would holler out, "Hi, Daddy," and when he heard us, he shouted back or waved his hand. He let us play the midway games as well and I still remember winning a kewpie doll there. The carnies chatted away to Dad and I used to think that they knew him from his work but really they were just being sociable. They were charitable to us too, and we often got a few free rides or a few free games. When I think about the noise of the rides—the loud amusement-park music, people screaming, and the general commotion of the fair—it must have been unnerving for Dad. Especially as he stood by rides, listening for our voices when the ride finished. But he took us to the fair each year because he wanted us to be happy and he wanted to do things with us like other fathers did with their children. If there was a way, he had the will.

My father took me to my first movie at the theatre to see Walt Disney's *101 Dalmations*. It was at the old Paramount Theatre on Barrington Street and it was just the two of us. I had popcorn and soda pop and it was all just so magical. I'm sure that for Dad listening to a Walt Disney children's cartoon movie was perhaps a bit boring, but he took me to the movie because he knew I would enjoy it.

When I was still in elementary school, I participated in a track and field event on the Wanderers Grounds, which was directly behind City Field where Dad worked on Bell Road. Dad stood at the back of the City Field property with his head cocked to one side listening for me to call to him. Just before my race, I called to him so that he would know I was running and when I finished the race I called to him again. Each time, he waved to acknowledge that he heard me. Of course, he had no idea where I finished but he heard the starter's gun and the crowd cheering as we ran the race. When he got home from work that day, he told me how much he enjoyed listening to my race and how proud he was of me even though I did not win.

The Canadian Council of the Blind, with help from the Lions Club, held summer picnics. An Acadian Lines bus would transport the visually impaired along with their families to a beach or lake near Halifax for the afternoon. I remember one picnic that my brothers and I attended with Dad. I was roughly eight years old. Mom wasn't with us because she had one of her migraine headaches. I cannot remember what beach we were at but there was a bit of a drop-off from the grassy picnic area to the beach below.

As I was playing, I saw a woman who was without sight carrying an infant as she walked in the direction of the drop-off. I ran back to my father who was sitting several yards away from the beach with some other adults. I told Dad what I was seeing. He instructed me to take him to the woman quickly. He took my hand and we ran toward the woman, but before we could reach her she and her child fell over onto the sandy beach below. I guided Dad down the slope to the woman and he helped her stand and checked with her to ensure that she and the child were not hurt. The woman had landed on her back. Both mother and child were fine, just a little shaken up, and the baby was crying. Dad later told me that the woman was clever because she instinctively twisted her body and fell onto her back to protect her child. He was impressed by her actions and visibly relieved they were both unhurt.

Point Pleasant Park in South End Halifax was my father's favourite place to visit and reflect. When he visited the park on his own, he strolled along the paths with his white cane, listening to the sounds of the wind in the trees and the birds chirping. As a youngster, I accompanied him to the park every opportunity I had. Dad enjoyed the smell of the woods and he told me that the autumn leaves as they lay rotting in the woods was one of his favourite smells. Each time we visited the park in the autumn, Dad would take a great big sniff of the air and say to me, "Can you smell the leaves, Sweetie Pie?" To this day it is a smell that triggers fond memories. I did not realize it then but Dad was teaching me to use all my senses to appreciate nature to the fullest. In autumn, I would collect brightly coloured leaves and show them to Dad for him to feel their shapes and sizes. When we returned home, Mom and I would press them between waxed paper for safekeeping.

It was not unusual to meet a mounted police officer doing his rounds while we were visiting the park. These officers knew Dad because the police stables were located adjacent to City Field on Bell Road. The officers always

chatted with Dad and they permitted me to pat the horse's nose. What a
thrill for me. In fact, Dad knew most of the Halifax City police officers and
he often received a lift home in a police car when they spotted him walking
or waiting for a bus. Our visit to the park almost always concluded with
a treat from the store, which is now called Point Pleasant Grocery, on the
corner of Tower Road right at the park entrance. Dad definitely overindulged
my brothers and me. Like his father indulged him as a boy, Dad took great
joy in doing so.

On one trip to the park, I brought along my little friend Jessie who lived
in the house across from our house on Cabot Street. We were eight or nine
at the time. We pranced along the paths through the park horsing around.
At Black Rock Beach, Dad allowed us to leave him so we could play by the
shallow water. He stayed behind on the beach listening to us playing. Jessie
and I ventured further away from Dad than we should have in order to stand
on the huge black rocks. We were having a great time dancing on the slimy
rocks until we edged too close to the water and we both slipped and fell in.
I don't think that we were playing where the water was over our heads, but
we panicked anyway and started screaming and splashing about frantically. I
know that Dad would have waded into the water to rescue us guided by our
voices, but a man who was nearby easily pulled us out and handed us over
to Dad. I wonder what he thought when he realized that Dad was blind.
We gave Dad an awful fright that day, yet he did not chastise us probably
because he was so relieved. There was no treat for us though and we had a
chilly ride home on the bus in our wet clothes. Dad had to explain to Jessie's
parents why she was soaked to the skin. That was very embarrassing to him
as he had been entrusted with Jessie's care and he felt that he had let her
parents down.

When my brothers and I had grown up and moved out of the house, Dad
travelled alone on the bus to Point Pleasant Park. He liked to sit on one of
the many park benches and just drink it all in. Sometimes he and Marjorie
would take a stroll through the park. On occasion he met his good friend
Janet Kitz there and they would enjoy the park together. Janet Kitz and Dad
became friends in the early 1980s when Janet began researching the Halifax
Explosion.

Point Pleasant Park, 2004. Eric examining a tree destroyed by Hurricane Juan in 2003. He was shocked and saddened by the destruction the hurricane wrought upon the park.

In 2003, Hurricane Juan tore through Halifax and devastated Point Pleasant Park. John took Dad to the park after it had reopened to the public so that Dad could examine some of the damage by running his hands over the downed tree trunks. He had to see for himself what the hurricane had done to his beloved park and he was shocked and overwhelmed with sadness at what he found there.

Mom and Dad did their best to ensure that we had everything we needed but not too much of what we did not need. Their lack of eyesight certainly did not hinder them in their ability as parents but Mom and Dad were always conscious of people critiquing them on their childrearing abilities because of their visual impairments.

We were taught that you didn't lie, you didn't steal, and you carried your own weight. And respect in our home was paramount. It was important to Mom and Dad that they raise us children to be respectful, responsible, contributing members of society.

Like all children, we did misbehave from time to time though. Mom and Dad did not yell at us. Punishment was generally being sent to our rooms to think about what we had done, and after some time we were set free after we apologized and acknowledged our wrongdoings. I'm ashamed to say that there were times when my mother sent me to my room for misbehaving. I would appeal to Dad for a pardon especially on summer evenings when all my friends were playing outside. On occasion, he rescinded the punishment and as I flew past Dad out the door I could hear Mom admonishing him.

Mom was the disciplinarian and we all learned very early not to test Mom's patience. She never put off a punishment for Dad to deal with when he came home from work and she never once said anything like, "Just wait until your father comes home." That may have been because she knew Dad wasn't much of a disciplinarian. Nevertheless if we misbehaved Mom dealt with it swiftly.

John staged a temper tantrum when he was very young in the Eaton's store on Barrington Street. Mom disciplined him right there in the store with a discreet tap on the backside. She did not hurt him but she got his attention and he settled down. On another occasion, when John was about seven years old, he refused to get off the trolley bus when it arrived at the Stanley Street stop on Robie Street. Mom knew the bus driver so she arranged with him to carry on to the next stop at Cabot Street, two blocks north of Stanley Street. Mom stepped off the bus, the doors closed, and off went the bus with John. When the bus stopped at Cabot Street, John shot out of the bus like a scalded cat and raced to Mom who was waiting for him at Stanley Street. Another lesson learned the hard way for John.

For my part, I had my mouth washed out with Sunlight soap for saying a naughty word when I was about seven. Worse still, I got caught playing chicken with cars. I was running back and forth across Robie Street with one of my friends and an astute driver chased us home. He came to the door and reported my actions to my mother. Steam was fairly coming out of her ears. I received my only spanking then and there and I know the driver must have heard me crying as he left. I will always remember Mom saying to me, "This hurts me much more than it will ever hurt you," as she put me over her lap and at the time I did not believe her.

Andrew got into trouble too; he was no saint. His most frequent misdemeanour was related to food or rather the concealment of food. In our house, there was no getting up from the table until your meal was eaten so Andrew, who did not like vegetables or potatoes, routinely hid them in his pockets, under the table, or wherever he could find a place to stash them. He also routinely forgot to dispose of them, and Mom usually found the stashed food later. Although his punishment was delayed, he was punished.

We really did not like to disappoint our father, and my brothers and I would fall completely to pieces if he ever became upset with us. We expected our mother to punish us when we misbehaved, but on the rare occasions that our father did, we were shattered. With me, it was only once that I received a feeble tap on the backside for being mean to Andrew and I deserved it. He was only a toddler and he loved to run from the kitchen to the front door of our house on Cabot Street. One day, I opened the front door as he reached it and out he tumbled onto the veranda. He wasn't hurt but he cried and I confessed right away when Dad asked me what happened. Knowing that my father was upset with me was far worse than the tap I received. I was devastated. On another occasion, I recall getting a lecture from Dad when I was about eight. We had been to a children's Christmas party at the Bedford branch of the Royal Canadian Legion where my father was an honorary member. One of Dad's friends was driving us home and he asked me how I liked the present Santa had given me. I was less than enthusiastic in my response. Dad told me there and then that I was ungrateful and that he was not happy with me. I felt miserable that I had disappointed my father.

When John was about ten, he had a disagreement with Mom after supper and stormed out of the house, staying outside until it became dark. He then tried to sneak in. Of course, darkness was no hindrance to our father and he was waiting for John. As soon as John stepped inside the house, Dad grabbed him, gave him a smack on the backside, and quite a verbal raking over the coals. Like me, John was devastated that Dad was disappointed with him. Dad was lenient on us with some of our childish behaviours but he would not permit disrespectful behaviour, especially toward our mother.

When Andrew was eighteen, he arrived home in the wee hours of the morning after partying on New Year's Eve. Dad wasn't happy and he knew that Andrew did not have a key so he locked the door on Andrew. When Andrew knocked, Dad answered and played coy.

Dad: "Who's there?"

Andrew: "It's me."

Dad: "What do you want?"

Andrew: "To come in."

Dad: "You might as well stay out at this time of night."

Dad's tough love was more humorous than anything but he was annoyed and Andrew knew it. Andrew did not have to spend the night out though; Dad let him in.

Our eye care was extremely important to Mom and Dad and we visited the optometrist routinely as children. I recall one visit when I was about ten. The doctor commented that I likely hid things on my parents and sneaked around them. I was offended and I told my mother what the doctor had said, adding that I did not want to visit that doctor again. Mom just chuckled though and she did not seem as concerned about it as I was. Yet she did not take me back to that optometrist again.

Mom was extremely clever, resourceful, and very organized. She had to be because it wasn't easy raising a family of three children with the challenges that she and my father faced each day. Mom and Dad did not believe in buying on credit so they didn't buy what they could not pay cash for. Mom could stretch a dollar thinner than most and she always budgeted and planned ahead, saving enough money to see the family through at least three months if Dad were to lose his job or if he was off work due to a strike. And there were strikes occasionally, but we never went without, thanks to Mom's money management.

Mom was a voracious reader of Braille books and magazines. She could read print with a magnifying glass, but as my brothers and I learned to read, she left reading print to us because she did not want us picking up her manner of reading print, which was slow and halting. In particular, handwriting was difficult for Mom to read. In time, it became more convenient for Mom to have us read handwritten and printed materials for her and Dad. Very little of what Dad was interested in reading was in Braille format, such as books about automobiles and auto mechanics, so of course we read any auto materials to him.

Mom was an extremely skilled knitter. She learned to knit from her mother and she acquired further skills while attending the School for the Blind. She knit everything from mittens and scarfs to elaborately patterned sweaters, Christmas stockings, and throws. There was nothing that my mother could not knit. Whenever Mom was knitting, she listened to her audiobooks, or talking books as she called them, from the CNIB Library.

Mom knit for her family but she also knit hundreds of baby sweaters, bonnets, and mittens for less fortunate children over her lifetime. Her legacy is definitely her Christmas stockings for which she won several first-place awards at the Canadian National Exhibition in Toronto. Each member of our family has a personalized Christmas stocking that was lovingly knit for us by Mom. When friends visited our home at Christmas time and saw our stockings hanging, they asked Mom to knit stockings for their family too. The demand for Mom's knitted Christmas stockings was tremendous, and they are now hung each year in so many homes. Mom was knitting right up until a few months before she passed away.

For as long as I can remember, Mom listened to CNIB Library talking books. Every few weeks, one or two books would arrive by mail. Mom listened to a variety of book genres but she particularly enjoyed non-fiction. As we grew older and left home, her free time increased and so did her consumption of talking books. Over the years, Mom listened to hundreds. She not only enjoyed the books but she believed that they expanded her knowledge on a variety of issues. The CNIB Library was an invaluable source of entertainment and learning for my mother and she and Dad generously supported the work of the CNIB Library through financial gifts, even leaving an endowment in their estate. Audiobooks for the visually impaired are now available at the public library.

Mom communicated with her visually impaired friends across the country by Braille and she had her own Braille writer. It is one of the treasured heirlooms that I kept, and is now proudly displayed in my daughter's home.

Even though Mom had very limited vision, she was an excellent cook and homemaker. Mom was brought up on a working farm where hearty meals with a healthy portion of vegetables were a necessity after a hard day's work. She was adamant that Dad should have a full supper each evening because he worked hard each day to put food on our table. Mom's cooking was not from recipe books; it was from memory. She cooked mainly German dishes or South Shore cooking as we called it, meaning South Shore Nova Scotia. She and Nanny made the most delicious homemade bread and pies and boiled dinners of meat, cabbage, and potatoes or sauerkraut, and pork chops baked with a dollop of molasses were family favourites. Dad always enjoyed a cup of tea and a dessert at the end of his meal. If I had one complaint about Mom's cooking, it was too many boiled potatoes.

Meals together were quality times when our family shared more than just food. Everyone participated in the conversation as we talked about the day's events or other family matters. There was much laughter. On rare occasions we dined out, and when we did we went to Cousin's, a neighbourhood restaurant that has been on the corner of Robie and Duffus Streets since the 1960s. Mom and Dad liked the homestyle meals there.

One of Dad's little quirks was his penchant for cleanliness, especially at the table. He examined his cutlery before he ate no matter where he was—at home, at a restaurant, or even at someone else's home. If any of the cutlery felt unclean, he asked for another. And he was fussy about his food too.

Without sight, he had to trust that his food was properly prepared, and if something did not taste quite right to him, he wouldn't touch it.

Dad's favourite food was fish. He often said that he could eat fish every day given the chance. He enjoyed all fish except cod and that was my fault. Codfish and potatoes with leaf lettuce salad was a regular staple at our house until the worm incident of 1969. Even though my mother was a very good cook, sometimes being a good cook is irrelevant. We were eating supper one evening when I saw what I thought was a worm in my father's fish. I told Dad and Mom. Now the worm may have come from the fish or from the lettuce but it didn't matter. That was it. Dad pushed the plate away and told Mom that he would never eat cod again. Codfish and potatoes never made another appearance on the Davidson table.

# Grandma Georgina

Sundays were days of rest and there was no work undertaken on that day in the Davidson household. Church played a major part in our family life. Sunday morning my father donned his best suit and tie for church and he remained dressed that way for the entire day. This routine was rarely altered throughout his life. We walked as a family to United Memorial Church, which was several blocks away. Often, someone would offer us a drive as we walked along. There were many Sundays that Mom was not with us because she was not feeling up to it.

We routinely entered the church through the side door behind the Kaye Street entrance. Dad always hung his hat and coat on the same coat hook along the stairway up to the church balcony. He counted the number of stairs until he reached the correct hook. My good friend Gail recalls how teary eyed her father would get as he watched us enter the sanctuary and make our way to our usual pew with me always holding my father's hand. Even though Dad could not see, he always held the hymnbook with Mom or with me while we sang. In later years, only Dad and I attended church together regularly.

In the afternoons, Dad visited his mother and sister Marjorie who lived together on Liverpool Street. The mother-daughter relationship between Georgina and Marjorie was very strong, a direct result of surviving the

Halifax Explosion together. Although Marjorie had suitors, she did not marry, forfeiting a life of her own in order to live with and care for her mother. Marjorie was a schoolteacher and principal at several Halifax schools throughout her career. The first school she taught in was Richmond School, which had been rebuilt after being destroyed in the Explosion.

Marjorie arrived at our house after lunch to drive Dad to Grandma's house. She always had a shiny new car and it was spotless inside. My brothers and I usually accompanied our father on these weekly visits when we were young. Dad wanted us to visit Grandma with him, as it was important to him that we knew our grandmother and that she knew us.

Grandma Georgina was not a particularly warm and coddling grandmother though. In fact, I found her intimidating. She believed that children should be seen and not heard so I sat quietly in the living room watching the interaction between Dad, Marjorie, and Grandma. There was always lots of laughter. Even at my young age, I could see the love Grandma had for my father. She always prepared an afternoon tea and fussed over Dad, folding a napkin on his lap and ensuring that he had his cup of tea and a plate of cookies placed properly in front of him. She seemed happiest when she was doting on Dad.

When I got older, I didn't visit Grandma as often, but I do recall one visit when I took my fiancé, John, now my husband, to meet her. Grandma, Dad, and Aunt Marjorie were sitting in the living room as usual. But Grandma did not acknowledge our presence at all. I was quite embarrassed and upset with her for her discourtesy. John and I excused ourselves and left. I did not see my grandmother alive again, which I will forever regret.

Annoyed with Grandma, I expressed my feelings to Dad. He apologized for her behaviour and he told me that I should not let it bother me. He said that Grandma was not always so abrasive but that she seemed to be getting cranky in her old age. He dismissed her behaviour as old age, but I think my father understood why she behaved as she did and he made allowances for her. He loved her unconditionally and he accepted her the way she was without complaint. He didn't spell it out for me then, but I believe he knew that Grandma's personality and occasional churlish disposition was a direct result of her harrowing experiences as a survivor of the Halifax Explosion.

Eric and his brothers Walter and Jim (l–r). Sisters June seated on left and Marjorie, 1941. Their mother, Georgina who never fully recovered from the trauma of the Explosion, could appear stern to the author.

My mother never visited Grandma Georgina's house and it was a rare occasion when Grandma visited our home. When I was about eight, I asked Mom why she did not come with us. She told me that she wasn't welcome there because Grandma had not wanted Dad to marry her. So there was an unspoken agreement between Mom and Grandma Georgina and they were rarely in each other's company. Although Grandma was a contrary mother-in-law, Mom seemed comfortable with the arrangement. Mom had empathy for Grandma for what she suffered during and after the Explosion. Although this strained relationship between Mom and Grandma put my father right in the middle, it did not adversely affect his relationship with either woman. Dad visited Grandma every Sunday regardless of disagreements or bad behaviour. Dad, Marjorie, and Georgina shared an impregnable bond that was forged when they survived the Halifax Explosion together. Doubtful anything could have severed it.

In the spring of 1975, Grandma Georgina fell down her basement steps, breaking her hip. While in hospital, she developed an infection from which she did not recover.

Aunt Marjorie was a wonderful aunt and we were all very fond of her. She and Mom had a great relationship too. Marjorie spent a lot of time in our house and there was lots of fun and laughter when she visited. Her sense of humour was like Dad's and she was fun-loving and kind. It didn't hurt either that Marjorie loved to shop, and when she visited us she brought treats for my brothers and me and quite often a small gift for Mom and Dad. Dad would sometimes chide her for spending money on gifts for him. But she enjoyed doing it and she was going to continue to shop for everyone regardless of what Dad said.

The Davidson family dynamic was a difficult one. While Dad and his siblings were close to their Williams cousins, they were less close to their Davidson cousins, other than Victor's children. Distance may have been part of it—James's family lived in Manitoba, Rachel's in the US, and Victor's in Saint John. Victor visited Dad whenever he came to Halifax, and when he passed away, left him a small inheritance. I do not recall my father speaking about his paternal grandparents; they died when he was a young boy. He did not know his Aunt Rachel either. When Rachel's family visited Victor, William, and Jeannie in New Brunswick, they did not come to Halifax. About ten years before my father's passing, our American cousins reached out and came to Halifax to visit Dad, as they had heard so much about him and wanted to meet him. We had many conversations over the years since, wondering why our respective grandparents did not communicate especially following the Halifax Explosion, but no one knows what caused the rift. It is all water under the bridge now for the Davidson family

We lived on Cabot Street until May 10, 1965, when we moved around the corner to a larger house on Prescott Street. My parents had been waiting for this house to come onto the market and when it did they were thrilled. The house was an attractive storey-and-a-half with a picket fence around the front yard. It had four bedrooms: two bedrooms on the main floor and two upstairs. The floors were hardwood. French doors separated the dining room from the living room, and there were lots of windows, making it bright and cheerful. This was my mother's dream house. The house on Cabot Street was becoming too small for a family of five and this new house afforded so much more living space that Nanny Zinck came to live with us too. Grandpa Zinck had passed away a few years earlier. Nanny lived with us for nearly twenty-five years before she passed away.

We weren't in the new house too long when I walked out of the kitchen into the back porch and found myself surrounded by flying ants. They were everywhere. This did not do my bug phobia any good and I emitted a few quality screams. Mom gave me a can of bug spray to kill the insurgents and Dad set out to track down the source of the outbreak. He found it was rotten wood on the back veranda so he got right to work and tore down the old veranda. Within a few days, Dad had built a new veranda and that was the end of the bugs.

Shortly after the bug incident Nanny made a mistake that nearly cost my parents their new home. She was making homemade bread and she turned on the oven to heat it up before placing the pans of bread dough inside. However, Nanny had a habit of storing food in the oven and she forgot to remove a Tupperware cake container from the oven before she turned the oven on. The plastic container melted and caught fire. The fire and smoke were so bad that Mom had to call the fire department, which promptly arrived and put out the fire. The smoke damage was mostly to the downstairs rooms but what a mess it was. Mom, Nanny, and I scrubbed cupboards, floors, walls, ceilings, and everything in between for weeks. My grandmother felt terrible and Mom wasn't too pleased either, but eventually we got the mess cleaned up.

The new property on Prescott Street did not have a garage so Dad arranged to have a two-car garage built. With the help of Ken Waterman and Harry Porter, Dad worked away on the garage. Ken and Harry were both navy men and antique-car-buff friends of Dad's. One evening, the men were working on the garage and it was getting dark so they decided to call it a day. The garage still did not have doors so all the tools had to be stored in the basement when the men finished for the day. When the ladder was taken to the basement, Dad grabbed the front and Harry grabbed the back. The door to the basement from the rear of the house opened to a rather steep flight of steps. Dad scooted down the basement steps, but as there were no lights on in the basement, Harry could not see and could not keep up with Dad. When Dad realized that Harry had almost fallen down the steps he said, "Gee it must be getting dark. I guess we should turn on a light." They had a good laugh at Harry's expense. Before long, the garage was complete and what a beauty it was. It had been several years since Dad had his own garage so he was thrilled to once again own one and he enjoyed spending evenings there chatting with friends or tinkering on his antique McLaughlin Buick.

In October 1968, Mom and Dad received the shocking news that the Halifax-Dartmouth Bridge Commission was expropriating their property along with others on Prescott Street for the Robie Street bridge approach to the A. Murray MacKay Bridge. They were so happy with this home and did not want to leave it but there were was nothing they could do. Mom was gutted to leave her dream house. My parents received approximately $20,000 for their lovely four-bedroom house with the newly built detached garage. The bridge approach behind their Prescott Street home is now called Massachusetts Avenue.

For roughly six months after our house was expropriated, we continued to live in it while Mom and Dad searched for another home. I believe they paid rent to the bridge commission during this period. Then in the spring of 1969, my parents bought a huge two-storey house on a double lot on Kane Street. The house was on the block adjacent to the Hydrostone district in North End Halifax and across from Halifax landmark Willman's Fish and Chips. The house had four large bedrooms and a bath upstairs and a massive country kitchen, a den, dining room, and living room downstairs. The house was built by the Halifax Relief Commission in 1921 as part of the post-Explosion reconstruction. The original owners had lived in the house since 1922.

Shortly after moving in, Mom and Dad had the entrance porch beside the kitchen converted into a pantry. Then Dad built two sturdy sets of shelves for the pantry and secured them to the wall. Although the kitchen was huge,

A photo of the family home on Kane Street near the Hydrostone area, which was built after the Explosion.

it was very outdated so Mom and Dad had someone install a new sink and build them new cabinets. A rocking chair sat in the kitchen by the window overlooking the backyard and Nanny Zinck usually occupied it. Although there was a garage on the property, it was dilapidated so the next project was to tear down the garage. Dad subsequently built a two-car garage with the assistance of Ken Waterman. This was the second garage they built together. Once Dad had his garage built, he had a buzzer installed between the kitchen and the garage. When Dad was out in his garage and Mom needed him for any reason, she would ring the buzzer and he would return to the house. This was a very convenient feature. Next, they had the front closet on the ground floor converted into a small bathroom so Nanny did not have to climb the stairs for her frequent trips to the bathroom. In time, this feature would prove beneficial to Mom and Dad as well.

In 1969, Dad and I went shopping for a clothes dryer for Mom. She had a washing machine but she had never owned a dryer. Mom hung the clothes outside on the clothesline. In the winter, our clothes froze solid and when she brought them in they were rigid. Mom had no idea we were shopping for a dryer and when it was delivered she was taken by surprise. She claimed that the dryer was a waste of money, but it was well used and the clothesline was never used again in winter.

Dad had a superstitious nature—he would never stay overnight in a house that anyone had died in and it was bad luck if a bird entered the house. On occasion, a bird did get into our house on Kane Street through the chimney flue and Dad would have to get that bird out of the house and set it free. The bird could not die in the house for that would bring bad luck to the household. I think he may have inherited his superstition from his mother.

A few years after we settled into the Kane Street house, the bridge commission offered to sell the expropriated Prescott Street house back to my parents. The garage Dad had worked so hard to build had been torn down but the house was intact. The house remains to this day although it has been much altered and no longer resembles the house we lived in so many years ago. Mom and Dad turned down the offer because Dad would have to build another garage on what little land was left, but more importantly they had no desire to live next to a busy thoroughfare listening to cars and trucks all hours of the day and night. While Mom never liked the house on Kane Street and the whole expropriation matter was a bitter memory for her, my parents remained there for thirty-seven years.

Within a few years of moving into the Kane Street house, Mom and Dad paid off the mortgage and owned their home free and clear. They had come a long way since buying their first house on Prescott Street approximately twenty years earlier and my mother must be given credit for this. While Dad was the breadwinner, Mom was the financial expert.

Christmas was always a wonderfully happy time for us. The first Christmas that I have a record of is Christmas Day 1957 when I was two and a half years old and we lived in the little house at 27 Prescott Street. I cannot remember that day, of course, but I love to listen to the reel-to-reel recording my father made on that day. The tape runs for over an hour and it is truly heartwarming. Mom and Dad are laughing and having such a jolly time and their voices sound so crisp and young. I can hear the pride of parenthood in their voices. Mom's parents are there as well and everyone is so cheerful. Hearing my own voice when I was a baby girl is fascinating. Mom gushes over the new chrome table and chairs she and Dad bought for Christmas. That table now stands proudly in my cottage kitchen. The chairs have long since disappeared. On the recording, I am walking around pushing my doll carriage that Santa brought for me and one of the wheels squeaks. Dad says he must fix that squeak. My brother John tries to get me to crawl onto his back so he can carry me around like a horse but I say no. Mom urges me to talk and encourages me to sing, "Twinkle Twinkle Little Star," but again I say no. Mom says on the recording that I like to draw on the walls with my crayons and pencils and that she spends a good deal of time washing down paint. Mom was certainly very tolerant. Dad tenderly coaxes me to come to him, "Come Marilyn, come here, baby," and when I reach him Dad speaks to me so lovingly and he chuckles. He asks, "Marilyn, whose girl are you?" I am sure he was expecting me to say Daddy but instead I say Nanny. John is a real chatterbox and he is romping around like a jumping bean. Then Dad starts playing his banjo and the music is melodious. It is quite possibly the best recording I have of my father playing his banjo.

Further in on the tape, Mom announces that it is January 7, 1958, and it is near bedtime for John and me. Dad is again playing the banjo, and John and I are dancing to the music. Mom says that this is our nightly routine. Of course, there was no TV in our home then so we had to entertain ourselves. The recording reminds me that I was blessed to have such loving parents and a happy home; it makes me long for the days when we were a young family and life seemed so simple. What a gem this recording is.

There had to be at least four Christmas parties that we attended each year when we were young. My favourite party was the CCB Christmas party, which was held at the old CNIB building on the corner of Almon and Gladstone Streets. There is a new building there now and the CNIB is located on the ground floor. I vividly remember our family walking from our house on Cabot Street all the way down Robie Street to the CNIB. There was an abundance of good food, lots of running around with the other children, and best of all a jolly, visually impaired Santa Claus. He was as exchanting as any other Santas we encountered as children.

Our Christmas party at United Memorial Church on Kaye Street was usually after church on the Sunday closest to Christmas. In those days, there were lots of children in Sunday school and the hall downstairs was buzzing with excitement as we waited for Santa to arrive. There was also a candy-filled Christmas party at the Bedford Legion. Finally, a Christmas party for the children of City Field employees at the Halifax Civic Workers Union building on Isleville Street. We were certainly spoiled when it came to children's Christmas parties.

The hunt for the perfect Christmas tree was a special event. There were several tree lots within walking distance of our house. Or if the Boy Scouts or the men of our church set up a lot to sell trees as a fundraiser, Dad supported them. Dad would take us with him to pick out the tree and it was always an evening expedition so it was dark and quite cold as well. Dad relied on us to pick out a tree. He'd ask us if the tree had any noticeable bare spots. Then he would gauge the height and breadth of the tree by physically examining it to ensure that it would fit in our living room. To me, we marched home each year with the most beautiful Christmas tree ever. Dad brought the tree into the basement and sawed off the bottom to fit snugly into the tree stand. The tree usually sat in the basement a full day to let the branches fall into place and for any moisture to dry. Then the next day Dad and John hauled the tree up the stairs and into our living room. After the tree was fixed into the stand, we told Dad if it was leaning although he could pretty much tell on his own by feeling the way the tree trunk fit into the stand.

Decorating the tree was a family event. Until we were old enough to do it, Mom and Dad strung the lights. Inevitably, there was always a bulb or two that needed replacement before the string of lights would work. My brothers and I worked to find the bad bulbs. Mom strung the tinsel one piece at a time because we were not patient enough to string it properly. My brothers and I hung the ornaments. It was a joyous time with Christmas music playing on the radio or record player and our traditional Christmas treats of clementines and mixed nuts, the kind that need the shells cracked open.

Mom and Dad shopped at Woolworths and the Metropolitan stores on Gottingen Street and at Zellers and Eaton's on Barrington Street for our Christmas gifts. Mom wrapped every present. They did a fine job of squirrelling the gifts and toys away because we never found gifts that were hidden for Santa to deliver. On one of their shopping expeditions in the late 1960s, when we lived in the big house on Prescott Street, Mom and Dad arrived home from shopping one night and they were in stitches laughing. They had their arms full of packages. They told us that as they walked arm in arm to the corner of Cabot Street and Prescott Street they both stepped onto an icy patch on the sidewalk. Mom went down first and Dad fell right on top of her, but somehow they managed to hang on to the packages. They said they must have looked like a right pair of fawns trying to get up without dropping their parcels or falling again. They couldn't stop laughing, and it was infectious.

The excitement leading up to Christmas Eve was palpable. In those days, the Salvation Army band often played at the end of neighbourhood streets in the evenings before Christmas. And quite often carollers from our church came to our door singing. We looked forward to these traditions. We went to church on Christmas Eve and once we returned home, our practice was to open one gift before going to bed. Cookies and milk were put out for Santa and then we eagerly got ready for bed and Santa's visit.

Christmas morning we got up bright and early, giddy with excitement and anxious to see if Santa arrived. Santa always managed to find our house and we were always happy with what he brought for us. We roused Mom and Dad first and, of course, they joined us for all the excitement of tearing gifts open. Once the gifts were unwrapped, back to bed went Mom and Dad until breakfast. Mom had only one stipulation and that was that no candy was to be consumed until after breakfast. Later in the day, the aroma of turkey dinner with all the fixings filled the house and in late afternoon we feasted on turkey and plum pudding.

Quite often, Dad worked back-to-back shifts at City Field in the winter. Halifax received some very bad blizzards in the 1960s, and when that happened Dad worked a fair bit of overtime. A co-worker brought Dad home in a snowplow or a grader and took him back after he had a good meal and a change of clothes. Sometimes we didn't see Dad for days because he was working or sleeping. We all dreaded it when Dad worked overtime during Christmas and luckily it didn't happen a lot but when it did, my parents worked around it. We still had a wonderful Christmas—we just delayed a few things like opening presents and Christmas dinner so that Dad could be there with us.

After we had all grown up and left home, my parents began an annual Christmas Eve tradition of listening to CBC radio for "Fireside" Al Maitland to read Frederick Forsyth's *The Shepherd*. The story is about an RAF pilot heading home to England from Germany for Christmas when fog sets in and all radio communication is lost. It is a tradition that John and I have carried on.

One of the most-loved Christmas presents our family ever received was an unexpected gift. A few days before Christmas in 1966 I went to Sam's Store, which was the convenience store at the corner of Robie and Stanley Streets. Sam's isn't there anymore but what a great little neighbourhood store it was. There on the doorstep sat a tiny black kitten with white paws mewing desperately and shivering with cold. Sam told me he did not know who owned the kitten and that it must be a stray. We did not have a pet at the time so I chanced taking the kitten home to ask my parents if we could keep it. To my absolute joy they said yes and I named the cat Purr Purr because of her strong purring. She was a gentle cat that liked to snuggle and in short order she became Dad's lap cat. Wherever and whenever Dad rested, there sat Purr Purr happily purring away while Dad petted her head and murmured to her, "Such fur, such wonderful fur."

In the first few years, Purr Purr managed to have four litters of kittens and we always found homes for them. Although she was a black cat, remarkably her last litter was five adorable, fluffy white kittens. Mom took on the role of nursemaid when Purr Purr delivered her first kitten on the basement steps. For each litter thereafter, Mom sat with Purr Purr as she delivered each of her kittens to ensure she stayed in her birthing box. After four litters, Mom said that was it, and Purr Purr was spayed.

Dad treated himself to lobster occasionally, and Mom banished him to the basement, as she didn't want the mess in the kitchen. As Dad headed downstairs, Purr Purr accompanied him, meowing all the way. If the cat happened to be outdoors, Dad called the cat to come join him. Dad laid newspapers out on his workbench before placing the lobster on it. When he began cracking the lobster, Purr Purr got louder and more aggressive. It was debatable who ate more lobster, Dad or the cat. Purr Purr was Dad's constant companion until the day she died twenty years later. Dad called me at home one day and asked me to come by to check on Purr Purr. A neighbour told him that the cat had collapsed in the driveway. Dad wanted me to confirm what he already knew. He couldn't bring himself to pick her up, knowing in his heart that she was gone. We buried her in the backyard of the Kane Street house. I found the cat in 1966 when I was eleven years old and I buried her for Dad in 1986 when I was thirty-one years old.

Dad missed having a cat, so shortly after Purr Purr died Andrew gave his cat Nick to Dad. Nick was a black cat with just a spot of white under his neck and he became Dad's lap cat too. Nick was quite a talker too and, like Purr Purr before him, he would meow in response to Dad's encouragement of "Such fur, such wonderful fur." Nick lived with my parents for roughly fifteen years. Amazingly, the cats never got in Dad's way or tripped him up. Dad loved his cats, and both Purr Purr and Nick provided many years of companionship and comfort.

# Peepers and Croakers

At any given time, you could look in Dad's jacket pocket and along with coins you would find a small wrench, a small screwdriver, a cotter pin, a banjo pick, and of course his pipe, tobacco, and matches. Dad smoked a pipe from his early teens until he was approximately ninety years old. Wherever he went, his pipe and a packet of Old Chum tobacco were tucked securely inside his coat pocket in case an opportunity arose for a quick puff.

In public, he was mindful of others and he would ask first if anyone minded him having a smoke before he lit up. When he finished smoking his pipe, he stashed it back in his coat pocket. I was always fascinated that Dad did not burn his fingers on the match when he lit his pipe. Andrew very aptly describes Dad lighting his pipe such that I can picture Dad right there in front of me.

As I think back to Dad lighting his pipe, I can almost smell the scent of his tobacco in the room. Old Chum was his preferred brand. It wasn't just an action—it was more like a ritual, the same way every time. Like a dance it had its steps and each step had its purpose. It began with filling the bowl with just the right amount of tobacco. The pipe bowl was inserted into the bag and filled. Next the lighting of the match. The match of preference was the wooden match that came in boxes of one hundred or more. Dad would light the match and hold it between his thumb and index finger so the second and third fingers could be placed against the pipe bowl thus positioning the flame directly over the bowl. A few good draws on the pipe would cause the flame to disappear into the bowl and then momentarily emerge again. Dad's head would then disappear into a cloud of sweet smelling smoke with the lingering odour of sulphur from the match. The match was then blown out but Dad held onto it and rotated it toward the palm of his hand so he could feel when it was extinguished before he placed it into the ashtray. He then sat back and, with the bowl held tightly in his hand and the stem between his lips just to the right side of centre, he would gently puff away in a total state of relaxation.

Dad knew Halifax streets better than most taxi drivers. He often gave visitors to our home instructions to their destinations, telling them of various landmarks to look for along the way. While this was nothing special to him, to others it was remarkable. Dad always knew where he was when he was travelling in Halifax. For instance, he knew when he was at the corner of Agricola and Young Streets by the smell of the hops or the sound of the flags flapping on the pole at the Oland Brewery. When he was in downtown Halifax or Point Pleasant Park, the sounds and smells of the harbour guided him.

More amazing though was that Dad was always cognizant of the street a vehicle was travelling on when he was a passenger in that vehicle. And he knew the direction the vehicle was travelling too—north, south, east, or west. If the driver made a wrong turn, Dad knew immediately and directed the driver back on course. In pretty much any drive over an hour, Dad tended to fall asleep and he would wake up while we were driving and know roughly where we were.

His ability to gauge the speed a car was travelling at while he was a passenger was uncanny. More often than I like to admit, Dad caught me driving a little too fast. He calmly said something like, "I think you're going a bit too fast, Marilyn," or, "What is the speed limit here now?" When Dad and his good friend Bob Huskins drove to Montreal's Expo '67 together in Bob's brand new 1967 Chev convertible, they were cruising along with the top down and Dad dozed off. When he woke up, he told Bob that they were moving along pretty swift. Bob was amused at Dad's subtle way of reminding him that he was driving too fast.

One pastime that my father enjoyed as much as his antique autos was preserving sounds and events with his reel-to-reel tape recorder. While anyone with sight appreciates beautiful scenery, my father appreciated sounds and smells. Wherever he went, his tape recorder went too. His recordings allowed him to relive the event the same as someone who watches a video of a treasured moment. Dad recorded my brothers and me as children learning to talk and while we were playing and singing. Dad recorded my piano recitals, Christmas mornings, birthday parties, peepers and frogs in the spring, trains, foghorns in Halifax Harbour, antique-car engines idling, and the list goes on.

Dad was particularly fond of recording "frogs singing" as he called it. His fondness for the sounds of nature was acquired as a young school lad when Sir Frederick regaled the children at the School for the Blind with readings from his own books about nature. My brothers and I often accompanied Dad on his evening frog-recording sessions. Sometimes we went by bus, but most times one of Dad's friends would drive us to a rural area outside the city where there was a large pond or swamp. We walked into the woods until we arrived at a good spot where there was a good chorus of frogs singing. Then, the recording would begin and we would be quiet. By the time Dad finished, it would be dark out. Sometimes, we had to rely on Dad to get us safely back through the woods to the road. On one such trip, Andrew nearly fell over something and Dad asked him, "What's the matter?" Andrew told Dad that it was very dark out and that he had tripped over something. For the remainder of the walk back to the bus stop as they approached an obstacle, Dad warned Andrew.

When we were licensed drivers, my brothers and I took Dad on his frog-recording sessions. As Dad aged, he found it more difficult to hear the peepers and croakers. Eventually he could no longer hear them at all and the trips to the ponds stopped. Dad listened to his frog and peeper recordings in the comfort of his favourite recliner chair for many years.

In the late 1960s, a little girl wandered into the woods behind her parents' home in Harrietsfield, just outside Halifax. The public was asked to help look for the lost child. This was long before Ground Search and Rescue operations were the norm. Dad very much wanted to help so off he and John went. When they arrived at the scene, there was a coffee truck on the road and a number of paths leading into the wooded area with many people heading in. Dad grabbed John's arm and said, "Let's go." It was very dark in the woods so John carried a flashlight. Dad asked him to look into the tree wells and under bushes while Dad got down on his hands and knees and searched under trees, swinging his hands back and forth along the turf. They searched for a few hours before calling it quits. They were both wet from crawling around the ground. On the way out of the woods, they met a man who told them they were going in the wrong direction so they took another path. After about ten steps, Dad stopped and said they were turning back to the original path, as he believed it was the right one. Dad's keen sense of direction got them safely out of the woods and they often wondered afterwards how long it took the man they met to find his way out. Navigating his way through the woods was not much different than navigating city streets for Dad. He relied on his other senses to direct him. The little girl was found the next morning but it was too late; she had died. Dad was very upset by the tragic outcome and was saddened about it for some time.

My parents had many friends both visually impaired and sighted. While sighted people can often be awkward with visually impaired persons, all of Dad's sighted friends were comfortable around him. They were also eager to assist him in whatever way they could—whether it was driving one of his cars for him or helping him build a veranda or a garage or driving him to the store for tobacco. Dad had a way of making people feel good when they were with him. Perhaps it was his positive attitude or his wonderful sense of humour, but when Dad made a friend that person was a friend for life.

My father relied mightily on his hearing. He could sense a person's disposition by the tone of their voice. He even knew when someone was present yet not revealing their presence to him. He had a sense about people after talking to them for only a few minutes. He identified people by their voices, so familiar voices he recognized instantly. People found it extraordinary that he could do this, but a familiar voice to someone without vision is like a familiar face to a sighted person.

Occasionally, someone would approach my father and say, "I bet you don't know who I am?" When it was obvious that Dad did not recognize the voice, most people told him who they were. However there was the occasional person who wanted to carry on the guessing game longer than they should. Although Dad was uncomfortable when he was put in that situation, he was always patient. The guessing game certainly upset me and my brothers because it went beyond a simple question of recognition to the absolute insensitivity of "You can't see me so try to guess who I am." As a young girl, there was little I could do but when I became an adult, I interceded when someone attempted to play the guessing game with Dad. I would immediately offer my hand in greeting and say, "I'm Eric's daughter Marilyn and your name is?" The obnoxious person was taken off guard and automatically took my hand and spoke their name. Game over, nipped in the bud. I was the recipient of a few curt glances when I interceded but I had rammed the message home. Ordinarily, my father would not approve of me interrupting, but in these cases Dad knew what I was doing and why I was doing it. He appreciated the interruption.

Mom and Dad had a large network of visually impaired friends locally and across Canada. Exposure to people with visual disabilities was common for us as children, and because of it, we were always comfortable around them and it gave us an appreciation for the difficulties that the visually impaired face. One visitor stands out for me. Her name was Jean Veinot and she was a bit older than my parents. Jean was deaf and blind. She was particularly fond of Dad too. He communicated with Jean by using tactile fingerspelling. She held out her hand, palm up, and Dad spelled or signed letters on her palm to communicate. Jean nodded her head in acknowledgement and often she laughed as the conversation went on. On one of her visits, she stayed overnight with us. In preparation for her visit, I learned the fingerspelling alphabet so that I could communicate with her too. She was very animated and thrilled when I spoke with her. Although Jean could not see, hear, or speak, she was an

Eric and Roy Kelly jamming ca. 1965. Eric is on banjo and Roy on piano. The two men were friends since their days at the School for the Blind.

amazingly cheerful woman. She unknowingly taught me at a young age that I had much to be grateful for.

Another who often joined us for Sunday supper was Eddie Horne. Eddie attended the School for the Blind when Dad was a student there. Eddie was musically gifted and he was a piano tuner by trade. Of course, he tuned our piano regularly. Eddie was also a very spiritual man and he preached at several local churches as a lay minister.

Dad knew several people who had been partially blinded by the Halifax Explosion, but he only knew one person who was completely blinded by it as he was. Tom Hinch and Dad were both small children when they lost their sight. They met at the School for the Blind and although Tom moved to the west coast when he finished his education, he and Dad kept in close contact for the remainder of their lives. Tom was a committed advocate for pensioned Explosion survivors and he went head to head with the Halifax Relief Commission, and in later years the Canadian Pension Commission, in an effort to increase pensions.

Dad enjoyed music and in particular he preferred bluegrass because the banjo is a prominent instrument in bluegrass. Dad was not a banjo virtuoso, but he could certainly pick a tune on the banjo and strumming his banjo was relaxing for him. Dad looked forward to any opportunity to bring out his banjo and jam with friends. "Watermelon on the Vine" was a favourite bluegrass tune and he often played it in his garage with friends who dropped by with their guitars. He was even known to crash the odd neighbourhood party and strum his banjo for the partygoers. Dad's siblings and their spouses often partied at our house too. Marjorie played the piano, Dad strummed the banjo, and the evening was filled with music and singing. My brothers and I went to bed many nights when it seemed like the house was rocking.

Many of these musical evenings were also shared with Dad's school chum Roy Kelly and another close friend Rod Trites who was also visually impaired. Roy played the piano, Rod played guitar, and Dad played his banjo. Music was a great part of their friendship and whenever they got together there was laughter. Roy and Rod called Dad "Dave," which was short for Davidson. The boys had some witty sayings that they shouted back and forth to each other. "Tiptoe through the tulips" was a common expression. "Down the cream" was a phrase that Dad and Roy used a lot. It referenced their school days when they used to secretly drink the milk left on the school steps by the milkman. The three friends barked "foghorn" back and forth to each other in their deepest voices mimicking the sound of a foghorn blasting. "Take your pension" was a greeting that Dad chirped to co-workers on a routine basis. These are just a few of Dad's funny little phrases he liked to belt out whenever the mood struck him, alone or with friends.

When telemarketers started to become a nuisance, Dad enjoyed having a little fun with them too. He switched roles with them and asked them questions. His favourite was to ask them if they would like to buy a forty-nine-cent broom. This was a reference to when he had tried to sell brooms as a student at the School for the Blind. The conversation never lasted too long before the telemarketer disconnected, likely thinking that they had a very confused person on the line.

My father entertained people with his banjo for many years at various social events, at Royal Canadian Legion dances in Bedford, at Antique Car Club and CCB gatherings and dances, in church variety shows, and seniors' residences. This was part of his volunteering. When I was ten years old, I sang while Dad played banjo at a Christmas concert at Brunswick Street United Church in central Halifax. I was nervous but everyone was very kind to me, so I mustered up the courage and sang. Dad told me he was proud of me for being so brave and I was thrilled.

As my brothers and I became licensed automobile operators, we travelled less by bus and more by car. Dad then bought modern cars for us to drive with the understanding that we were to chauffeur our parents whenever they needed us to. When John got his licence in 1967, Dad bought an early 1960s Morris Oxford station wagon. We toured the Cabot Trail in Cape Breton and across the ferry to Prince Edward Island in the Morris wagon. Mom and Dad particularly enjoyed the Woodleigh Replicas in Burlington, PEI. The replicas were scale miniatures of UK landmarks such as Dunvegan Castle, St. Paul's Cathedral, Shakespeare's birthplace, and so on. My parents knew they would never travel to the UK to experience the real sites, so the replicas were the closest they would get. Dad examined the replicas with his hands, which gave him an idea of the grandeur of the architecture of the original landmarks. Mom enjoyed visiting the Anne of Green Gables museum because she had read *Anne of Green Gables* as a young girl.

In 1971, when I turned sixteen, Dad bought an early-1960s Austin Cambridge with standard shift for me to learn to drive. Uncle Walter taught me. When I got my licence, Dad bought Walter's 1968 Plymouth Fury II for a family car. We still had the '68 Fury when Andrew got his licence. My brothers and I learned to drive on standard shift cars so we could drive Dad's antique autos. I recall driving the 1924 Studebaker in downtown Halifax and having to stop for the traffic light on the steep Cornwallis Street incline at Barrington Street. I was extremely nervous about coasting backwards, but with Dad's reassurance I held the Studebaker steady and we proceeded forward without incident when the light turned green.

In 1975, the National Film Board of Canada produced *Just One of the Boys*. The cameraman Mike Mahoney was himself a North End Halifax boy and as a young lad he delivered newspapers to our house. Mike witnessed my father working on vehicles and he was so inspired by Dad that when he decided to make his first film, he chose Dad as the subject. He pitched the idea to the NFB and it was immediately on-board. Mike had the utmost respect for my father, and he told me that Dad had a great sense of humour and was always very generous and accommodating with his time during the tedious filming process.

Mike recalled Dad telling him that he was looking forward to seeing the Rockies when he visited John in Calgary. Like so many others, Mike was struck by Dad's use of the word "seeing." Years later whenever Mike saw Dad walking along a city street, he would stop and offer Dad a ride. "Hi, Mike, how are you?" was Dad's usual response. Mike was always amazed that Dad could recognize his voice.

The crew spent roughly one year following my father and filming him. They filmed him at home working in the garage on his antique Studebaker, at an antique car show, and while he was at work at City Field. I have shared this film with friends, colleagues, and most recently with my fellow members of the Halifax Explosion 100th Anniversary Advisory Committee. Anyone who watches it is struck by Dad's ability to live the life that he did. The film has been used as a teaching tool for some years now by staff at the Nova Scotia Community College in their Automotive Service and Repair Program.

When I watch the documentary today, I am overcome with pride as I see Dad stride with confidence from the house to his garage as I have seen him do so many times before. He looks so young to me and I realize just how much I miss him still. It is emotional for me. There is a segment in the film where Dad is being driven along the street in his Studebaker and some children holler, "Hi, Mister Davidson" and it warms my heart. They knew that Dad could not see them if they waved, so they yelled their greeting.

Dad was on his way to an antique car show and the film crew followed him there. In the film, Dad speaks with some people. He feels a car and tells the owner, "That's a dandy car…I imagine you can make pretty good time with it." The car owner appears excited about Dad's opinion. "You'd be interested in the engine," he says as he reaches to open the hood.

Dad tells the interviewer that he can remember things from shortly after the Explosion, including his father taking him to areas where there was still debris lying about. "Sometimes, I think I can remember before, but that is just imagination," he says. Dad told me he remembered his father taking him to Richmond School and Grove Presbyterian Church some time after the disaster. He said he remembered walking and crawling through the debris with his father and that it was much like walking through a pile of kindling wood. He said his father told him that the congregation had just purchased a new organ before the Explosion and they examined the ruins of that organ together. Dad also told me that for some time after the disaster

Eric reassembling or rebuilding a carburetor at Citadel Motors in 1945 at the start of his incredible career.

he was frightened of the sound of sirens but that, other than those recollections, he did not remember anything from the Explosion itself. I think that was a blessing.

Dad is shown backing the 1924 Studebaker out of the garage and comments that he restored the car from the frame up and that when he got the car it was all rust. Dad points out that rust does not feel any better to him than it looks to a sighted person. Early in the documentary, Dad tells the interviewer that he would buy "an occasional car" and that he once got a REO for two dollars, "and it ran!" Dad thought that was quite a good deal. Dad fixed these cars and sold them. "It wasn't that hard to do," he tells the interviewer.

Both my brothers, John and Andrew, chose careers in automobile mechanics, which is hardly surprising given that they spent so much time with Dad as he restored his antique cars, and they were with him on many of his barn-snooping adventures too. My brothers and I inherited Dad's fondness for antique autos and we have all had our own collections over the years.

By the mid-1970s, my brother John was living and working in Calgary and I was working in Halifax. I thought of moving to an apartment as many of my friends did but I could not bring myself to leave my parents then. I am sure they would have accepted it as a rite of passage for me, but I viewed it as abandoning them. From a very young age, I felt a responsibility to assist my parents and by the time I was a young adult they relied on me for everything from simple housekeeping and yardwork to assisting them with their financial and legal matters and so much more. To leave them and move into an apartment did not feel right to me.

In 1975, I married John Elliott in United Memorial Church, and Dad walked me down the aisle. Now I had no choice. I moved to New Glasgow with John but every weekend he and I returned home to stay with Mom and Dad. When John went to Regina for six months as an RCMP recruit in 1976, I returned to live with my parents. Our first posting following his graduation in 1977 was Antigonish, Nova Scotia, and our weekend routine of driving home to Halifax resumed. In reality, I missed Mom and Dad and I needed them as much as they needed me. And so I was never separated from my parents for any more than a few hours' drive for the five years John and I were posted in Antigonish. John was posted to Halifax in 1982. Although we did not live with Mom and Dad, we were in and out of their home practically on a daily basis. I was fortunate that John loved my parents and wanted to be involved in their lives with me.

By the early 1980s, Andrew moved to Calgary and my parents became empty nesters. As John, Andrew, and I each bought our first homes, Mom and Dad generously gifted us the funds we needed for our down payments. They were pleased to help each of us make that first major investment.

My two children were born in the late 1970s not long before Dad retired. As was Dad's habit, he fretted while I was pregnant and when I delivered each of my children he called the hospital almost every hour. He just could not help himself. He was thrilled to be a grandfather and to once again hold an infant in his arms and gently brush his lips over their tiny heads and murmur, "Kiss a head." Mom and Dad were happy to have the little ones in the house and they sometimes had the children for an entire weekend while John and I were off to a curling event.

In January 1980, before Dad's retirement, I broke my ankle. Andrea was fifteen months old and Matthew was only a month old and both the children were in diapers. I was in a cast and walking on crutches so I could not look after my babies when John was at work. The babies and I moved in with my parents for several weeks. Dad took a two-week vacation to help Mom and me look after the children. My grandmother Zinck was still living with Mom and Dad, and it wasn't always easy having four generations living under one roof, but we made it work. Mom and Dad and even Nanny were a tremendous help and they all enjoyed having the babies living with them. We certainly livened up the house.

My parents' relationship was one of deep respect. They never raised their voices to each other and if they had disagreements they held them in private because I never witnessed a row between them. What my brothers and I did witness were displays of affection. Dad often helped Mom with the dishes after supper and he'd give her a little canudle and say, "Whoofie, whoofie," then laugh. Mom would just say, "Eric, behave yourself" and sigh. These little displays of endearment were common.

There is a misconception held by many in society that the blind are helpless. Many times people told me they were astonished that my parents were able to raise a family given their visual handicaps. While some aspects of parenting may have been more difficult for them because of their visual impairments, my parents were very able to raise us. My brothers and I realize how fortunate we were to have parents who loved each other and who loved us unconditionally.

# A Passion for Antique Autos

I have detailed pictures in my mind of every car I've ever worked on. I can clearly visualize each as I need to, but I've never seen one, that I can remember.[12]

My father was in his element when he was puttering on his antique cars. Dad's antique auto hobby started in 1953 when he hitchhiked alone to Moncton, New Brunswick, a distance of approximately one hundred and fifty miles, to buy a 1927 Springfield Rolls Royce Phantom 1. He bought it as a parts-only car, but within a few years he had it in fine working order and he used it for many day trips. In August 1955, Dad received a letter of thanks from the City of Halifax for participating in the Natal Day Parade: "Your entry of a 1927 Rolls Royce Limousine was an added and unusual attraction to the Parade this year."

The Rolls Royce was a big car and it filled the little Prescott Street garage. As there was not always someone present to assist him, Dad often backed the Rolls Royce out of the garage on his own in order to work on the engine and make adjustments. Occasionally, he permitted John to sit on his lap when he drove the Rolls back in.

12 Eric Davidson quoted in Shea, "He's Not Just Any Mechanic."

A garage was a necessity for my father. Furthermore, his garage had to be organized. It could not be cluttered with toys and household items for Dad had to be able to move around easily without tripping over things. An integral part of Dad's garage was his workbench, which he built for his garage on Prescott Street in the early 1950s. It was a heavy and solid workbench of four-by-four and two-by-six board lumber bolted together. It had a shelf below for storing tools and equipment and a vice attached to the front left side. Various engine parts were assembled or disassembled on top of the workbench. It moved with us to each property except Cabot Street where the workbench went to the rental garage on Duffus Street Extension. Dad also built a sturdy shelving unit for his basement. The shelf had many cubbyholes in it for Dad to organize small engine parts, various washers, screws, tools, and whatever items he might want to find at a later time. Like the workbench, this shelf moved with us to every house and it is now a permanent fixture in my own garage, a fond reminder of my father's carpentry skills.

Dad's basement workshop was almost a replica of his garage and there was structure and order to the basement workshop as there was in his garage. Dad found it very frustrating to be searching for misplaced tools or parts. He sometimes had to reprimand my brothers when they did not replace a tool properly. When a washer or small piece Dad was working with got away from him and settled where he could not find it, he called on us children to find the errant piece.

The Kane Street basement had one thing though that his other basements did not have. Shortly after we moved there Dad came into possession of an old wringer washer. Dad never worked on a vehicle without wearing coveralls over his clothing. They collected all manner of vehicle fluids and grease from top to bottom and front to back as Dad slid under vehicles on his dolly or leaned over fenders to work on engines. Dad washed his coveralls by hand in the set tub in the basement of each of our homes. Once he acquired the wringer washer, he again did his own laundry, feeding the coveralls through the wringer himself. Then he hung the coveralls on the clothesline outside to dry. Dad used the washer for more than thirty years.

Eric's prized 1921 McLaughlin Buick pictured in front of the Prescott Street home that Mary was so fond of. Year: 1966 or 1967.

Dad had three large red metal mechanic's tool cabinets, one for his garage, one for the basement, and one at his workplace, City Field. Each drawer held different tools of the trade and all of my father's tools were of high quality, mostly Snap-On. Like the workbenches, the tool boxes were orderly and organized. Dad identified all of his tools by touch. Some tools such as feeler gauges, which are used to set the sparkplug gap, required closer examination. To select the correct size feeler gauge, he ran his fingers back and forth over each gauge until he found the correct size.

Both his garage and his basement workshop were meeting places for Dad and his friends, the boys. While he was still working, co-workers would stop by in the evening or on a Saturday. After he retired, they dropped by for a lunchtime visit, bringing their lunches and spending an hour chatting with Dad. And then there were Dad's antique-car enthusiast friends who visited him regularly to chat about all things automotive. It seemed that hardly a day went by that someone didn't drop by to visit with Dad while he was tinkering away in the garage or the basement. Sometimes, they brought alcoholic refreshments. Dad enjoyed a beer but he rarely had to go to the liquor store himself to get it. He had a few select friends who did beer runs for him. He never asked me or my brothers to buy alcohol for him when we reached the age of maturity. Mom did not care for alcohol, so Dad kept his beer tucked away in the basement and he drank it warm. This comedic arrangement between my parents never varied and there was never a beer cooling in our refrigerator.

Dad's ability to establish an engine's mechanical problem by sound was uncanny. He simply tilted his head and listened to the engine running either on idle or the engine revving. He could identify the vehicle manufacturer by the sound of the engine too. He knew whether the car was a Ford, Chev, or Dodge and he said that Dodge vehicles had the most distinctive engine sound.

Dad routinely repaired vehicles for people. Between fixing other people's cars and working on his own antique cars, Dad was busy most evenings in his garage. Frequently, friends and acquaintances dropped by to have Dad "look at their car," which meant listen to their car to pinpoint and repair the problem.

On occasion though, someone would show up while we were still at the table eating supper. Dad would politely tell the person that he would finish his supper then meet them outside. He respected Mom too much to leave the table and he preferred to eat his supper hot not cold. After supper, he went to the basement, donned his grease-covered coveralls, and attended to the visitor's car. Dad never asked for monetary reimbursement from anyone who asked him to repair their vehicle. A case of beer may have been issued in trade now and again though. Conversely, if anyone did a favour for Dad, he repaid them financially or in kind. It was not in my father's nature to accept charity.

Many evenings it was dark outside when Dad worked on vehicles in the garage. The darkness was not an issue for him, but visitors often asked him to turn on the lights. This was an ongoing joke with Dad and some of his closest friends.

Over the years, Dad owned and restored many antique cars. In addition to the 1927 Rolls Royce Phantom 1, Dad's auto rebuilds or restorations were a 1921 McLaughlin Buick Touring, 1924 Studebaker, 1922 REO, 1925 Paige Limousine, 1947 Buick Roadmaster, a 1934 Rolls Royce Silver Wraith, and a 1935 Rolls Royce. There was a 1927 Model T, but Dad only restored the engine not the entire vehicle as it was a flip vehicle, one that he bought, fixed up the engine, and then sold for a modest profit. The early cars started by electric starter but if the battery was weak, Dad started them by cranking them. This was strenuous and it involved inserting a crank handle into the front of the car below the radiator and turning the crank with all his might to turn the engine over and start it manually. I do not recall Dad ever having a car towed home.

Dad liked the Rolls Royce engines because they would start on the spark advance. The spark advance and hand throttle were levers on the steering wheel and could be used as a manual cruise control. The spark advance was used to advance the ignition on the older cars, making the engine run smoother. Dad became very knowledgeable in this area. He soon became known locally as the expert in Rolls Royce engine repair, thus earning him the nickname the "Rolls Royce Man."

Dad acquired two of his Rolls Royces with the assistance of his good friend Ken Waterman. Ken was a pilot for the Canadian Navy, flying off the *Bonaventure*, Canada's only aircraft carrier. He went to England often and on two occasions he found a Rolls Royce for Dad and had each shipped back to Halifax. Ken was a frequent driver for Dad and it was Ken who was driving Dad's Studebaker in the National Film Board documentary.

The 1934 was the first Rolls Royce that Dad had shipped from England sometime in 1960. It was a 25-30 series, big and heavy, and an extremely nice vehicle to drive in. It was a very opulent automobile with a window between the front and rear compartment and an intercom system from the back seat to the driver. The steering wheel was on the right-hand side. There was a cigar lighter on one side of the back seat and a perfume decanter on the other. There were cushions and mirrors on both sides of the back seat and a bearskin rug on the rear floor. The interior was appointed with rosewood and the upholstery was velour. The driver's compartment was full of instruments and levers and leather upholstery. There were curtains on all of the windows in the rear compartment and this made for a great changing room when we went swimming at the beach. It had a trunk on the back with fitted suitcases inside and there were twin side-mount spare tires and jacks to lift the car built into all four corners. Under the driver's seat was a complete tool kit.

This Rolls Royce was a family favourite. In 1961, our family drove in it to a wedding in Seaforth along the Eastern Shore beyond Dartmouth. Ken Waterman was our driver that day too. On the trip home though, we got a flat tire and Dad and Ken had to fix it by the side of the road in the dark. I was terrified that we would not get home but the tire got fixed. I was fast asleep by the time we arrived home so Dad carried me into the house and to my bed.

In December 1963, Dad had a 1935 Rolls Royce shipped from England and Andrew still has the bill of lading for this car. It cost $384.82 to have the car shipped to Halifax by the Cunard Steamship Company Limited. I can only imagine what that might cost today. Dad often took John with him to the rented garage on Duffus Street Extension when he worked on this Rolls Royce. Dad rebuilt the engine in that garage. John cleaned and painted parts, read manuals for Dad, and helped assemble whatever Dad was putting together.

Often they worked into the evening and darkness would set in, so John sat on the running board of the car and read Dad's auto manuals by flashlight. The engine had complicated linkages and components, but Dad took it all apart down to the crankshaft and put it back together again. The only reference he had was John reading him the Rolls Royce manual. Dad boiled pistons on our stove so he could install the wrist pins and the connecting rods. Then, for a week, he installed one piston at a time with John positioned on top of the engine and Dad underneath. It took Dad about a month to reassemble the engine and John recalls that it was impressive to see everything complete. Dad had that engine running as well as it did when the car was brand new, and a square-sided nickel balanced on edge on the radiator while the engine was running at curb idle would not vibrate or fall off. The engine would start on the spark advance and run so quietly that people often did not know it was running.

In 1964, at the Halifax Antique Car Show when the judging was being done, John was asked to start the engine. He started it with the spark advance, and the engine started as it always did, silently. The judge asked again for John to start the engine and John told him the engine was already running. Dad got full marks for that one.

Seven-passenger touring cars were the cars that Dad preferred though. The McLaughlin, Studebaker, and REO were all touring cars. The 1921 McLaughlin Buick was Dad's favourite antique car because it was a Canadian-built vehicle. He bought the McLaughlin, which was a seven-passenger open touring vehicle, in Edmundston, New Brunswick, in the early 1960s. We used and enjoyed this car more than any of the other cars Dad owned over the years. We all have so many memories of riding in the McLaughlin in Natal Day parades, trips to beaches and lakes, and runs to Wolfville, Hantsport, and many other rural communities with the Halifax Antique Car Club.

For many years when Halifax held a Natal Day parade, Dad entered his antique car and my brothers and I had the fun of riding in it. We thought we were royalty as we sat in the back seat waving to the crowd of people watching along the route. Sometimes one of my little friends accompanied me. The open touring cars had no windows, only side curtains, which were never on during a parade. There were always a number of Dad's good friends who were eager and willing to drive his vehicles. Dad sat up front in the passenger seat with his head stuck out the side listening to the car's engine to ensure it wasn't overheating. As the parade was always the first weekend in August, sometimes it was quite hot and it was not uncommon for the car's engine to overheat on the stop-and-start parade route. Dad was prepared for such happenings with his tool box and a spare jug of water for the radiator.

Because Dad owned the 1935 Rolls Royce and the 1921 McLaughlin Buick at the same time while we lived on Cabot Street, he needed to rent two garages. The second garage was on Summit Street and that is where the 1921 McLaughlin Buick was stored. Dad and John did a lot of walking back and forth to that garage. Dad removed the body from the frame so they could clean and paint the frame and chassis and repair some rotten wood in the body. He sanded the wood and John did the painting. They installed new body-mount rubbers and reinstalled the body back onto a freshly painted chassis. Dad rebuilt both running boards and completely went through the fuel system and then installed new tires on the front.

On one of our outings, Dad had a new person driving who didn't understand older engines and against Dad's advice he pushed the McLaughlin engine too hard and burned a connecting rod. Dad was not pleased and that person never drove another of Dad's cars. Of course, Dad repaired the engine, and the car ran as good as new again. Like all of his restorations though, Dad sold the McLaughlin to buy another restoration project. He forever regretted selling that vehicle. Ironically, several years later Dad and Andrew were on a car-hunting trip in Oshawa, Ontario, when they came upon the McLaughlin covered in years of dust in an old barn. Dad tried to buy it back, but the owner would not sell it.

Over the years I wrote many letters for my father in search of antique auto parts in Ontario, the United States, and as far away as England for his restoration projects. Parts such as carburetors, head gaskets, pistons, fuel pumps, and even tires for those old cars were not readily available in Nova Scotia. Each restoration had its own unique complications and each would generally take a few years for Dad to complete.

The 1947 Buick Roadmaster was a beast of a car and what a sweet ride. Dad bought the car in Alberta in the early 1970s, and Ken Waterman drove it to Halifax. Somewhere in New Brunswick, the Buick struck a moose. The right front fender, headlight, and chrome trim, as well as the windshield, had to be replaced and the passenger door had to be repaired. Otherwise, the car was intact. Not so the moose.

The 1924 Studebaker is the restoration that I remember most. It was a rusted skeleton of a car when it appeared in our backyard on Kane Street. It had been stored in Woodstock, New Brunswick, prior to arriving in Halifax. Dad restored it from the ground up. He had a body shop sand and paint the car and he had Maritime Canvas Converters make a new roof, using the old one as a pattern. He overhauled the engine and did the rest of the restoration himself. The Studebaker eventually ended up in Norway of all places.

Dad never got attached to the 1922 REO. It was difficult getting parts for it and he genuinely just did not like the car. However, it was his final restoration, and my brothers and I formed a sentimental attachment to the car. Andrew owns it now but he rarely takes it out on the road because the REO cannot get up to the minimum speed required these days.

Given his keen interest in antique autos, it is appropriate that Dad was a founding member of the Halifax Antique Car Club in 1963. In the early 1960s, he and a few like-minded pals got together and discussed the idea of forming a club. They were all old car buffs restoring cars. The formation of the club gave them a place where they could gather, exchange information, and help each other in their restoration projects. Dad served a term as president in 1965. My brothers and I had a lot of fun accompanying Dad to the annual car show at the Halifax Forum and the car club cruises to places such as Windsor and Truro. Sometimes, there would be up to twenty cars cruising together on the secondary roads. Passing motorists would wave and beep their horns in approval as we chugged along. The Halifax Antique Car Club took off like a race car and it is still very active today.

In 1963, the Rotary Club sponsored the first antique car show at the Halifax Forum. Every year since, there has been a show. The car show was quite a thrill for me and my brothers. The excitement of spending a few days at the Forum running about with the other participants' children was something we looked forward to each year. My father was always the centre of much attention from the attending media and from the car show patrons. Everyone wanted to chat with the blind mechanic and watch him as he tuned his car or adjusted the timing on someone else's vehicle. Dad entered his Rolls Royces in the car shows and he did the stationary nickel display. Over the years, Dad acquired quite a collection of trophies for his cars. Upon receiving a trophy once, he commented to his friend and fellow car club founder Bob Huskins that he hoped he got the trophy for what he did with the car and not because of his handicap.

Dad and his car club friends scoured the Maritimes looking for barn finds, which were antique cars that had been stored in garages or barns for decades just waiting to be plucked for restoration. They'd get a tip that an antique vehicle was in a barn somewhere and off they'd go. Dad was welcomed wherever he went and people were always amazed with his automobile expertise. Dad became friends with collectors from across Nova Scotia, New Brunswick, and beyond.

Bob Huskins often accompanied Dad on these searches in rural Nova Scotia and New Brunswick. On one such trip, he and Dad were driving along a rural dirt road in Pictou County with miles of nothing but woods. They were looking for a farm where a steam car from the early 1900s was stored. Bob had no idea where to turn off but as they crested a hill Dad told him to slow down as they must be close. Shortly after, Bob spotted the property they were looking for. Bob was floored that Dad had been able to direct him on a road that neither of them was familiar with. I suspect that prior to the trip Dad had been given verbal directions and, using his great sense of direction, was able to guide them to their destination.

On another barn-hunting expedition, Bob and Dad were checking out a Model A Ford that was for sale in Halifax County. The owner of the car had claimed that it was in original condition. When they were returning home, Dad told Bob that the car had been in an accident. Bob asked Dad how he knew that, and Dad explained that one of the headlights was closer to the radiator than the other headlight. Bob had not spotted the headlight issue, but Dad caught it right away during his hands-on examination of the car.

Bob and Dad had many memorable outings together. In later years, Dad and Bob didn't get out together as much but their friendship never waned. Bob plowed my parents' Kane Street driveway for several winters, arriving in the wee hours of the morning and gone before my parents arose. Mom and Dad were pleasantly surprised when they awoke to a clear driveway but they wondered who the mystery plowman was. In time, they learned that Bob was the kindly fairy.

I hitchhiked with my father on an antique auto scouting trip to Greenwich, Nova Scotia, when I was no more than seven or eight years old. Dad wanted to visit a gentleman who owned an antique touring car hidden away in his garage. This man lived alone in a few rooms of an old weathered two-storey house. We stayed in the kitchen the entire visit and I sat quietly while Dad and this gentleman spoke of cars. Dad, of course, could not see what I saw. The kitchen table was littered with stacks and stacks of old newspapers and the place was in a total state of disarray. It was in the fall of the year and it was cold in the house. I couldn't wait to leave and once outside, I described the messy kitchen to my father. He told me the man lived alone and Dad felt sorry for him because he had no one to help him keep the house tidy.

The barn snooping and car hunting started for John when he was about seven years old, and he and Dad hitched a ride in a Volkswagen microbus over the south mountain from our grandparents' home in Mahone Bay to Middleton. From there, they hitchhiked down the Valley to Bridgetown where they met up with Ken Waterman. Dad bought an old Chev that day. It was in bad shape but Dad managed to get it running. They started for home and ended up in a ditch when a tire blew. Ken fought the steering wheel with all he had, but the car went into the ditch anyway. They were pulled out of the ditch by a passerby and subsequently fixed the flat tire and carried on.

On another trip, John and Dad travelled by train to Harvey Station, New Brunswick, for a ride in a steam car. Dad knew a gentleman there who had a number of antique cars and a Stanley Steamer was the flagship of his fleet. They were able to take the Steamer for a drive and the gentleman allowed Dad to examine it from stem to stern.

John's next trip with Dad and Ken was to a residence in Antigonish County. Dad had learned of an 1899 Locomobile in Antigonish County so off they went in Ken's newly painted 1956 Buick Roadmaster. As they turned off the road and onto the property, there were large posts on either side of the driveway indicating that at one time this was a grand estate. The road was barely passable for a car and after a long slow drive down the driveway they came into a clearing with an old house. Almost immediately, dogs appeared from everywhere. John was terrified. The dogs were all over Ken's car, their claws scratching the paint. Ken was in a panic about his car. An older gentleman came to the doorway of the house, swinging a large piece of wood about the size of a baseball bat. He gave a loud roar and the dogs disappeared. Dad, Ken, and John got out of the car and walked up to the Locomobile, which was beside the house. It was just a buggy with a boiler and cylinders and a seat with a tiller for steering. The men discussed the possibility of buying the vehicle but the owner wouldn't sell. They returned home with nothing but Ken's badly scratched car. When John was sixteen, he made a return trip with Dad to try and buy the Locomobile. This time there were almost no dogs to speak of. The old fellow still did not want to sell the Locomobile and it remained sitting where it had been years earlier.

John was on a barn hunt with Dad in Edmundston, New Brunswick, when Dad had a very embarrassing incident with his prostheses. They were rushing to catch the train home to Halifax and Dad could not find his prostheses. He was annoyed at himself for misplacing them. At the hotel's front desk, Dad tried to explain to the female clerk who spoke only French that he had lost his eyes somewhere in the room. Between Dad's inability to speak French and the woman's lack of English, it was a lost cause. Dad and John left the hotel thinking the prostheses were gone for good. Fortunately, when they were seated on the train, John found Dad's eyes. Dad had mistakenly put his glass eyes in John's coat pocket instead of his own. Dad went to the bathroom to wash the eyes and put them in.

On many occasions, I observed my father backing his antique cars out of or driving them into our garage but I never had the pleasure of seeing Dad drive a car on a beach or a deserted road as he did in his younger days. John was more fortunate. John was in one of the Rolls Royces when Dad slipped behind the wheel and drove along a deserted beach with Ken guiding him. They drove about a quarter of a mile before Dad turned the car around and brought it back to where they had started.

Garth Scott, a good friend and early member of the car club, fondly remembered Dad at the time of his passing. Garth wrote this tribute:

Eric was kind, clever, friendly and humorous. Whenever you met Eric whether in his garage, at a car show, or on the street he was always positive, uplifting and humorous. I could spot Eric on a city street, pull up to within one hundred feet and shout tiptoe through the tulips and Eric would shout back, Garth, how the hell are ya? What a guy, what a friend, what a survivor, what a genius.

The Halifax Antique Car Club set up a financial award in my father's memory shortly after he passed away and each year the Eric Davidson award is presented to the top student in the Automotive Technician program at the Nova Scotia Community College. Displayed on the wall at the Akerley campus is the Eric Davidson plaque.

# The Golden Years

Life holds very great happiness and interest for me. Ninety more years would be too short for all the different things I have in mind to do. I guess the poet who wrote about God taking away eyesight so that the soul might see had something very real to say.[13]

When Dad retired from City Field in 1980, he and Mom became more active in the Canadian Council of the Blind, which is a national self-help consumer organization of persons who are blind, deaf-blind, and visually impaired. The CCB strives to improve the quality of life for persons with vision loss through advocacy, peer mentoring, social and sporting activities.

Mom and Dad started bowling again, which was something that they had only done occasionally since their courting days. Members of the local Lions Clubs volunteered with the CCB bowling league, coaching and scorekeeping. Dad found bowling somewhat frustrating because more often than not he came away with a poor score but he bowled because he knew Mom enjoyed it. Mom and Dad both attended many of the CCB sports weekends, which were held in a different Maritime or Maine location each

---

13 Eric Davidson quoted in Alice Bardsley, "Light in an Endless Night," Family Herald. Nov. 6, 1958.

year. Mom competed in bowling and cribbage and Dad in bowling. Mom was very involved with the CCB and the planning of these events. She served several terms as the Halifax Club president and as Maritime Division president. She worked to improve accessibility for the blind/visually impaired and she strived to have the provincial government provide the same treatment to them as offered to other handicapped groups.

Mom and Dad also took up square dancing. Lions Club volunteers taught the blind and visually impaired to dance. While Dad enjoyed dancing, Mom entertained it mostly to please Dad.

Dad became very involved in volunteering following his retirement. He volunteered at the Camp Hill Veterans Hospital from 1983 until 1999, spending an afternoon each week visiting with resident veterans, listening to their stories and chatting. The veterans looked forward to his visits. He also volunteered at the Northwood seniors' residence in North End Halifax for over twenty years. At Northwood, he played his banjo as a member of the Fun Band, entertaining the residents once a week with lively music from the 1930s and 1940s. Dad was an avid blood donor for several decades, periodically recognized by the Canadian Red Cross Society with milestone awards.

In the early 1980s, Dad and Mom began taking an annual trip to Calgary to visit my brother John and his young family. In Alberta, Dad loved the mountains where he could breathe the mountain air and where he could hear the river running down the canyons.

For Dad, travelling on land by car or by train was enjoyable. However, flying was an unpleasant experience for him. Dad had a very real fear of flying because he had difficulty understanding the aerodynamics of getting a huge aircraft into the air and flying. While he had an idea of what a plane looked like by examining model airplanes, it was a mystery to him how anything that immense could get off the ground. Dad always had an alcoholic beverage or two before flying to relax him.

One trip to Alberta in the mid-1980s, Andrew accompanied Dad as they travelled by train to visit John and Ken Waterman who was living in Alberta at that time. When the train stopped in a small Manitoba town, Dad and Andrew strolled into town to explore. Andrew thought the train was there for a lengthy stop. They weren't in town very long when Dad said to Andrew,

"Listen, that's our train whistle blowing, we better get back to the station."
Dad recognized the whistle blow as a call for passengers to board the train.
They ran back to the station with Dad holding tight to Andrew's arm and
they arrived there just as the train started to pull out. The conductor saw
them running and stopped the train to permit them to board safely. If Dad
had not heard the whistle and recognized what it meant, they would have
been left behind in Manitoba.

On the same trip, Dad and Andrew were booked to fly home. When they
arrived at the airport though, the airplane had been overbooked and only
one seat was available. Dad seized the opportunity to opt out of flying and
insisted that Andrew take the seat. Ken drove Dad to the train station and
Dad leisurely rode the train from Calgary to Halifax alone. However because
he and Andrew had separated at the airport in such a hurry, Andrew took the
wrong suitcase, leaving Dad with nothing but dirty clothes. It was a three-day
journey and by the time Dad arrived in Halifax, he had three days' growth on
his face and he looked like a pirate. But he was totally relaxed.

On various visits to Calgary, Dad and John rebuilt a Model T engine
and chassis that John had sitting disassembled in his garage for some time.
Father and son got the old car put back together and running like a charm.
Then they drove the Model T chassis up and down the alley behind John's
house looking like the Beverly Hillbillies out for a drive.

On another visit to Calgary, Dad had the opportunity to examine a
hot air balloon, which he found intriguing. The balloon had to make an
emergency landing very near John's house. Before the envelope had deflated,
John was able to get Dad close enough for him to get an idea of the size of
it. He examined the basket and the workings of the hot air balloon. Dad was
always eager to learn something new, so that was quite a thrill for him. He
had no desire to take a ride in the balloon though.

Dad and Mom both became licensed ham-radio operators in 1980.
Several of their sight-impaired friends were ham operators and many of
them lived in other provinces so Mom and Dad saw this as an opportunity
to communicate with them on a regular basis. One of these friends was Tom
Hinch, who also lost his sight in the Halifax Explosion. Tom lived in British
Columbia and he and Dad kept in touch by phone or by mail. However,

when Dad became a ham-radio operator, he and Tom communicated on a more regular basis. Another of Dad's frequent ham-radio contacts was his good friend Roy Kelly who was living in Dartmouth. Ham radio brought friends like these together where distance kept them apart.

In 1984, John and I were living in Lower Sackville when I became very ill and had to be hospitalized for ten days. I knew that Dad, ever the worrier when we were ill, would be anxious to visit me, but I also knew that my condition would be extremely upsetting for him so I asked John to plead with him not to come until I was feeling better. This was very difficult for Dad but he did as I asked. After five days, I was on the road to recovery. In short order, Dad arrived at my bedside with an egg sandwich that Mom had made for me and a container of chocolate milk. He was very much relieved when he was able to visit me and he visited with me every day thereafter until I was released.

Nanny passed away in 1989. Mom and Dad were now alone in that huge house. As Dad visited his mother on Sundays for so many years, we fell into a routine of visiting Mom and Dad as a family on Sundays. Our visits were suppertime visits and it has become a humorous family memory about how often Mom served roast beef and how quickly my children tired of it. For a change, I would occasionally prepare scallops for Dad, John, and me. Mom and the children had Kentucky Fried Chicken on those occasions.

My children were fortunate in that they spent a great deal of time with Mom and Dad and forged a strong relationship with them. As a teenager, Andrea visited them almost daily. She often accompanied them to a variety of Canadian Council of the Blind events and she volunteered at the CCB sports weekends. Mom often referred to Andrea as her second daughter. Andrea's relationship with her grandparents steered her into her career as a vision specialist working with visually impaired children at Atlantic Provinces Special Education Authority in Halifax and with the Calgary Board of Education. In her own words, Andrea sums up her relationship with Mom and Dad:

Sunday dinner at my grandparents' house was roast beef or KFC. I wish I could go back to that kitchen with all of us sitting around the table chatting and simply enjoying being with each other. I would gladly eat a second helping of roast beef if we could all be there together again. After dinner while Mom helped Nan with the dishes, Grandad retired to his chair and smoked his pipe. I loved the smell of his tobacco. Grandad usually gave Matt and me money to go to the corner store to buy him a pack of tobacco and some sort of "sweet." He let us have the change to spend on candy. We loved it! We bought lots of candy with the leftover money. Grandad liked to spoil us.

As I grew older, I began to assume many household chores that Mom did for Nan and Grandad. It just seemed to be the natural thing to do, natural in that if you love someone you help them in any way you can. And boy did I love my grandparents. I painted the garage and the front porch. I cleaned the windows in the spring, mowed the lawn in the summer months, raked leaves in the fall, shovelled in the winter, helped with the laundry, and cleaned the house top to bottom every two weeks. When I mowed the lawn and raked leaves, Grandad always insisted on helping me by holding the garbage bag open while I filled it with leaves or grass clippings. I looked forward to my Saturday morning cleaning routine for Nan and Grandad. Their house was very modest and they were not messy people by any means but they could not see crumbs, dust, etc. Grandad rested in his favourite chair listening to CBC and smoking his pipe while I cleaned all around him. Sometimes he would say something back to the radio but most often he slept. His jaw would drop and small snores would emanate. Even though they knew that I was happy to help them, they would not allow me to do the chores without being paid. It was a pride thing for them. They did not accept charity and would have been offended if someone saw them in that way.

After I finished cleaning, we had lunch, which quite often was fish and chips from Willman's across the street. We chatted away just sharing in each other's company. We talked about school, upcoming events, family, the news, anything and everything. Their home felt like my home. Neither Nan nor Grandad would quip in with advice or lecture me about anything; they just listened. No matter what I did in my young adult years, they loved me unconditionally and they never passed judgment. They just listened and I loved that about them. Once, when my parents were away, I broke up with a boyfriend. Instead of being alone in our house, I ran up to my grandparents' house and cried in Nan's arms. She just held me, softly whispering, "My dear girl, it will be okay." There have been many times when I have longed for that hug and reassurance again.

On occasion, I had to search around Grandad's radio table or look under his chair to find one of his artificial eyes. With age and muscular atrophy, his eye would fall out and it was impossible for him or Nan to find it. Nan very discretely told me that his eye was missing so we would not embarrass Grandad. When I located it, I returned it to Nan for her to wash and give to Grandad. He was very modest about those things.

Grandad loved it when I decorated their house each year for Halloween. I passed him decorations to examine and feel with his hands as I put them out on the porch or on the lawn. He meticulously felt the fake spiders and ghosts but I knew better then to give him any fake snakes as Grandad hated snakes! I also made cardboard tombstones, which he particularly enjoyed because of the funny sayings I put on them. As I passed out candy to the children on Halloween, Grandad sat nearby and I described the various costumes to him. He quite enjoyed hearing the children saying, "trick or treat!"

After earning my teaching degree, I was a substitute in the Truro and Halifax areas. I was volunteering at the CCB Sports Weekend when I was introduced to the director of APSEA, Atlantic Provinces Special Education Authority. We talked briefly about the programs APSEA offered and that they also provided a scholarship to students interested in pursuing a master's degree in Special Education for students who are blind/visually impaired. I jumped at the opportunity and applied. I was comfortable in the visually impaired community. I often attended or volunteered at CCB events with my grandparents and as such I knew many visually impaired people. Nan always played her cards close to her chest, but the day that I told her I was accepted into the master's program she cried. She was very proud of me. She gave me a big hug and said, "my girl." That was what she always called me.

I spent the next two and a half years working with APSEA while working on my master's. This was exactly the field I wanted to be in. I had an appreciation for the struggles students with disabilities faced and I wanted to be a part of a program that was assisting them with their education within our ever-changing world. My work in Calgary, Alberta, introduced me to students who reminded me of my grandparents. I often told them about my grandparents and encouraged them to lead a full life as my grandparents did.

Upon his retirement, Dad spent many afternoons and evenings smoking his pipe while relaxing in his recliner in the sitting room at the front of the house. Beside the recliner was a small table that held the telephone, his tape recorder, radio, and ashtray. On the recliner was a throw with the design of a leopard. The throw was precious to my father because Marjorie had given it to him. It only left the chair when it was being washed. While relaxing in his recliner, he listened to his personal taped recordings or CBC radio. His favourite program was *Cross Country Checkup* and he sometimes called in to the program to voice his opinion about the topics being discussed.

In the warmer months, it was routine for Dad to sit outside on the front veranda smoking his pipe. Neighbours would come by and chat and others would simply say a quick hello as they walked by. The enclosed veranda afforded the space for a lounge chair or a cot and it was quite common for Dad to have an afternoon or early evening snooze there.

In the early 1980s, I had a Siberian husky named Timber. Dad often took Timber for a walk and they often ended up at Dad's favourite watering hole, the Lions Head Tavern on Sullivan Street. Sometimes, Dad was challenged for having the dog in the tavern but he responded that the dog was his Seeing Eye dog. Anyone who knows anything about Siberian huskies knows that they are not Seeing Eye dogs, but the staff were fond of Dad and he was never asked to leave.

On one occasion when Dad took Timber for a walk, he decided to be a daredevil. It was a silent night in winter with the snow falling gently. Dad and Timber had been gone for some time when they arrived back at the house with Dad huffing and puffing and Timber panting. Dad said he had gone to Novalea Drive and listened to make sure there were no cars coming. Then he and Timber got in the middle of the road and he commanded the dog to run. Timber pulled Dad down the street with Dad sliding on his boots. It must have been a spectacle to see. Dad had a great time that night.

Throughout his life, it was customary for Dad to check in with his family by phone on a regular basis. Dad called Grandma and Marjorie each night and he kept in close touch with each of his siblings. When Walter spent winters in Florida in the early 1970s, they communicated by sending cassette tapes of their newsy conversations back and forth by mail. Long-distance phone calls were still too expensive. As my brothers and I moved out of our parents' home, Dad called us in the evenings and we chatted about the day's events, sharing a giggle or two. How I miss those nightly chats.

In 1983, the Halifax School for the Blind was closed and plans were underway to demolish it to make way for a parking lot for the Victoria General Hospital. Dad and Mom were upset. They both credited the School for the Blind for preparing them to lead productive and independent lives. For several days in January 1984, Dad stood out in the cold weather to record the demolition. Mom was too upset to accompany him. She could not bear to see the school where she had formed so many friendships and happy memories torn down.

On January 17, 1984, Dad was standing on Tower Road sidewalk facing the south side of the school. The crane operator saw Dad recording and asked him if he had attended the school. He permitted Dad to examine the one-tonne ball at the end of the twenty-two-metre boom. He explained to Dad how the ball swung into the structure to knock it down. He told him what part of the building he was working on and he detailed each part of the operation. At the end of the conversation, he told Dad that he was happy to meet and speak with him. As Dad recorded, the ball smashed into the girls' section of the school where there were still some beds and dressers visible. Each day as he stood there recording, bystanders who were watching the proceedings spoke with him, often asking him if he had attended the school.

On January 19, 1984, Dad was recording from South Park Street sidewalk, and CBC *Information Morning* reporter John Mason stood with him and interviewed him. Dad told John when he attended the school and he also told him about the school as he remembered it. In turn, John kept Dad informed about the progress of the demolition. I do not know if John Mason was formally interviewing Dad that day for CBC or not but here is an excerpt from Dad's recording:

John: "Do you record other sounds with your tape recorder?"

Dad: "Anything I can get. Someday I'm going down to the waterfront when it's foggy and record the sounds of the ships and foghorn down there."

John: "How do feel about the school being torn down?"

Dad: "I feel a little sad about it, it's a landmark and it's a shame they're tearing it down like that."

John: "There's an old metal fire stairway leading up to that dormitory. Did you stay in those dormitories?"

Dad: "Oh yes, I was there."

Dad was one of the most successful graduates of the Halifax School for the Blind, and he is still held up as a role model for students by teachers at the current school, now named APSEA, the Atlantic Provinces Special Education Authority.

Where once the school had so proudly stood there is now a parking lot, which is part of the QEII Health Sciences complex. A few decades later, graduates of the school raised funds and in 2012 they erected a Halifax School for the Blind monument on University Avenue where the gates to the school once stood. Although my parents had passed away before they could see this project completed, they generously supported the erection of the monument. I was present when it was unveiled on September 28, 2012.

I recall attending a concert at the School for the Blind with my parents in the mid- to late-1960s. I remember being struck by the grandeur of the building but I will never forget how touched I was by the students. Even at my tender age, I was brought to tears as I watched them perform. I have always had a soft spot in my heart for anyone who is blind, especially blind children.

While she was researching the Halifax Explosion in the early 1980s, well-known Halifax historian and author Janet Kitz and my father became close friends. They shared many common interests, in particular Point Pleasant Park, which was a favourite retreat for them both and where they occasionally met for a walk and a chat. Dad is featured in two of Janet's books about the Halifax Explosion, *Shattered City* and *Survivors: Children of the Halifax Explosion.* My father held Janet in high regard because she did so much to preserve Halifax history, both for the Explosion and for the park. He often remarked that Halifax was fortunate that Janet arrived here from Scotland or much of our history would have been forgotten.

In 1987, when the Maritime Museum of the Atlantic mounted their first Halifax Explosion exhibit, *A Moment In Time*, a huge tactile photograph of my father was displayed on an entire wall. The photographic display and a brief story about Dad remain today as part of the museum's current permanent Explosion exhibit, *Halifax Wrecked.* Anyone who is visually impaired can examine the photo by running their hands over it.

In 1991, Dick Drew, a Canadian radio executive authored a book *The Canadian Achievers* based on his syndicated radio program of the same name. The book featured inspiring stories about ordinary Canadians and their outstanding achievements. Eric Davidson's story is one of the stories, along with those of Wayne Gretzky and Clifford Chadderton to name a few.

In 2002, Dad was awarded the Queen's Golden Jubilee Medal on the occasion of the fiftieth anniversary of the accession of Her Majesty Queen Elizabeth II to the throne. The medal is awarded to Canadians who have contributed to public life. He received the award for giving to his community through his many years of volunteering. Dad was humbled by this recognition.

The following year in 2003, a six-part television series about growing up in Canada in the twentieth century was produced for the History Channel. The series was called *Growing Up Canadian* and Eric Davidson was one of the featured stories. Dad has been the subject of media attention over the years and there are simply too many to list; suffice to say his remarkable life has been well documented.

When his sister Marjorie suffered a stroke in the late 1990s, Dad visited her in hospital nearly every day for two years until she passed away. Even though she could not communicate with him, he faithfully sat beside her bed chatting away to her, believing that she understood everything he said. It pained Dad to see Marjorie so helpless but he was comforted just to sit with her as she lingered in that state. Dad was extremely saddened when she passed in 1998. Brothers Walter and James predeceased him as well. Only June outlived Dad and the siblings remained close during their long lives.

On the occasion of my parents' fiftieth wedding anniversary in 2000, my brother John wrote a tribute to Mom and Dad. An excerpt from that letter:

> Our family shared many special moments together and to put one above the others is too hard to do. Walking together home as a family from church, Christmas mornings spent together in our living room, antique car shows and parades where I felt like a prince, to the trip we took over the Cabot Trail and PEI in the little Morris station wagon. Though all of these are good memories, I have to say that my most vivid memories as a child are the ones where I was learning life's little lessons. As a child, I thought I had special parents but it was not until I was a parent myself that I realized just how special you are. As parents you had a vision of how we were to be raised and you never wavered. You guided me. You saw what I did not. Most of all, you were always there.

In 2005, my parents sold their home on Kane Street and moved to Berwick in the Annapolis Valley. John and I had moved to Kentville the previous year due to job relocations. We encouraged Mom and Dad to move in with us then but they declined saying they did not want to be a burden. John and I resumed our weekly visits to Halifax to be with Mom and Dad just as we had done when we lived in Antigonish so many years earlier.

Within a few months though, my parents decided it was time to sell their house and move closer to me. Dad was ninety years old and Mom was eighty-five. They moved to Orchard View in Berwick, an assisted-living complex with an adjoining nursing home, Grand View Manor. It is right across the street from the United Church camp where we had such a wonderful time in the summer of 1962. Orchard View is in a quiet country setting with pleasantly appointed apartments. Mom and Dad were welcomed there by the residents and staff, and they quickly adapted to the new lifestyle of living in a one-bedroom apartment. This was a major transition for them; however, they were very comfortable in Orchard View and they were only a few minutes away from me.

The move to Berwick was a very positive transformation for my mother. She was like a butterfly leaving the cocoon. A full-course meal was provided at noon in a sunny dining room where they ate with other residents. The only meals Mom had to prepare were breakfast and something light such as soup or sandwich in the evenings. Their rent included a weekly cleaning of their unit. Mom visited with other ladies simply by walking from her apartment to theirs. Prior to leaving Halifax, there hadn't been as many visitors to their home, as many of their friends had predeceased them. Their new neighbours frequently dropped by for visits. Mom was content there. She did not miss the house on Kane Street.

Dad, on the other hand, missed living in Halifax. Even though he enjoyed visiting the Valley, the North End had always been his home and he found it difficult at times adjusting to the fact that he no longer lived there. For a few years before the move, Dad was not able to get out and walk, ride the buses, or even putter in his garage, so he had effectively been house bound. Yet, in the Valley he felt somewhat detached from the city he loved so dearly. He particularly missed his garage and he often took the opportunity to tell anyone that he used to have a fine garage and lots of tools. He would have preferred to remain living in North End Halifax, but like so many challenges he faced in his long life, he met this move head-on too. It was important to him that Mom was happy and he always put the happiness of others before his own.

In 2006, my son Matthew who is a member of the Canadian military was deployed to Afghanistan for a six-month tour of duty. At that time, Matthew was a soldier patrolling outside the wire in harm's way. We were all worried for him, but Dad was extremely upset. He could not understand what was going on in the world at that time and he worried and fretted until Matthew arrived home safely.

As Dad's hearing became less acute and as his dementia worsened, his independence started slipping away. He did not like that at all. It gave him a feeling of helplessness that he was not used to. This was possibly one of the lowest times of his life. Dad always said he wanted to live to one hundred but he wanted to do it with a sound mind and body. In late 2007, he began to have frequent falls and his health had slipped to the point where he needed around-the-clock nursing care. Mom was becoming exhausted too. We discussed with him the imminent need for full nursing care. He realized his health was failing and that he needed heavy care and he did not want to burden Mom. Unfortunately, heavy care was not provided in Orchard View. Dad would have to move next door to Grand View Manor.

When the actual day arrived in May 2008 for Dad to move, Mom and I were heartbroken. We were not ready for this. It was quiet as my mother and I wheeled Dad down the hallway to his new accommodations. When Dad asked me where we were going, I broke down. I was quietly sobbing and unable to speak. Mom immediately sensed my distress. She took Dad's hand and we walked along in silence. Without a doubt, this was the most difficult thing I ever had to do in my life.

When we arrived at his room, a nurse greeted us and welcomed Dad, saying how happy they were to have him in their care. Dad, who had faced so many challenges in his life, graciously accepted this transition, commenting that he did not want to wear Mary down. Grand View Manor is attached to Orchard View by a corridor, which meant that Mom and Dad could still be together each day. They would however be separated at night for the first time in their fifty-eight years together. It was a major adjustment for them both but we were all extremely thankful that they were only a few doors apart. Aunt Marjorie's leopard throw went with Dad. It provided comfort to him during the day and it covered him at night.

As I was still working, I visited with Dad evenings and weekends, as did Andrew. John routinely travelled from Calgary to visit our parents. We took Dad for walks in his wheelchair when it was warm outside. When it became difficult for him to eat on his own, we helped him. It is very sad to witness our father who was so fiercely independent lose his independence. Dad received outstanding care at Grand View. The staff treated him with respect and they did their utmost to keep him comfortable. Dad was only in nursing care for fifteen months. He passed away on September 9, 2009, at ninety-four years of age. My parents had been married for fifty-nine years.

Dad's funeral was held in Halifax at United Memorial Church. The church was filled with people paying their respects. Dad would have been humbled to see so many present. His dear friend and best man, Arch Rasley was there. Janet Kitz spoke fondly of Dad to the mourners. When Matthew took the pulpit to speak about his grandfather, he haltingly said, "I've jumped from a helicopter and I've been shot at, but this by far is the hardest thing I have ever done." John (my husband) gave the eulogy filled with happy family memories and stories of Dad's remarkable life and his positive outlook on life. John shared with everyone present that when he applied for the RCMP he was asked whom he most admired and looked upon as a role model. His response to his interviewer was Eric Davidson.

Members of the Halifax Antique Car Club lined the street in front of the church with antique cars in a show of respect.

A Davidson relative from New York wrote to us saying, "In our family Eric has always been a folk hero having overcome his blindness and able to live the life that he did."

Dad's passing was reported by various Canadian media sources locally and nationally, including the *Globe and Mail* in Toronto and CBC Radio in Vancouver. Halifax city council observed a minute of silence at their September 15, 2009, meeting to honour Eric Davidson.

Dad was laid to rest near his beloved parents and sister, Marjorie, at Fairview Lawn Cemetery in Halifax.

In November 2012, the City of Boston mounted an exhibit honouring Eric Davidson at City Hall to coincide with the annual Christmas tree–lighting ceremony on the Boston Common.

On June 21, 2013, Halifax regional council approved the placement of my father's name on the sports field at Fort Needham Memorial Park in North End Halifax. The J. Eric Davidson Sport Field is in the same park where the Halifax Explosion Memorial Bell Tower sits and where the Explosion commemorative service is held each December 6. This is a very fitting tribute to such an iconic survivor of the Explosion and lifelong native of North End Halifax.

Mom passed away almost two years after Dad. She was ninety-one. I was with Mom when she passed, and when I think of our last moments together I see Mom as a young woman, not an old woman. It is odd the games one's mind plays when dealing with loss.

The task of dispersing my parents' possessions was difficult yet rewarding. My brothers and I kept a great deal of our parents' things. I had the diamonds from Mom's wedding ring made into a charm, as the ring itself was worn thin from sixty-one years of continual wear. I think of Mom daily when I use her favourite set of Friendly Village dishes. I also have her wedding dress and knitting needles, as well as one of Dad's fedoras. Among other things, Andrew has the 1922 REO and John has Dad's gold pocket watch.

Before she died, Mom gave me instructions for some of their material possessions. Mom's most precious possession other than her wedding ring was her binder of Braille knitting patterns. She wanted the knitting patterns to be given to someone who was visually impaired. As it happened, Andrea worked with a visually impaired woman in Calgary who was an avid knitter, so we decided that this woman should have Mom's Braille patterns to use and enjoy. She was thrilled to receive them.

Musician Alan Doyle of Great Big Sea fame became the owner of one of Dad's banjos. The banjo had been bequeathed to Dad by a friend. Yet, Dad rarely took it out of its case. He was somewhat superstitious and he did not feel comfortable playing that banjo, so it stood in his closet year after year. We advertised the banjo locally and we were contacted by a friend of Alan Doyle's who told us that Alan had an identical banjo stolen. They thought that we may have been the thieves when they first saw the ad. I explained the story behind the banjo and why we were selling it and the banjo found a new home. Recently my daughter-in-law met Alan in St. John's and he told her that he has put the banjo to good use and that he has played it on some of his albums. Dad would be well pleased that the banjo is making such fine music.

# The Halifax Relief Commission Pension Fund

The Halifax Relief Commission was established by the Government of Canada in January 1918 to assist victims of the Halifax Explosion. It was incorporated by an Act of the General Assembly of Nova Scotia in April 1918. The commission was entrusted with approximately $27 million in public and private funds received as aid from national and international sources. The Government of Canada was the major contributor, supplying $18 million.

The commission's immediate mandate was to provide emergency housing and relief to Explosion victims, to clear and rebuild the devastated area, to establish health programs, and to arrange for the care and education of blinded survivors. The commission disbursed approximately $4 million in emergency aid and $20 million for damage claims and reconstruction. More than three hundred units were constructed in the area west of Fort Needham within the Hydrostone and surrounding streets.

The Relief Commission was further entrusted by the Government of Canada to oversee the management of pension funds for survivors who suffered life-changing permanent injuries and for women who had been widowed. Survivors were offered either a lump sum or a monthly pension for life. The monthly pension was much smaller, so many chose the lump sum and in later years regretted their decision.

Nova Scotia Archives photograph shows the construction of Hydrostone housing in 1919. Hennessey Court (now Hennessey Place) units at left and Kane Court (now Kane Place) units at right.

Blinded or sight-impaired children did not qualify for a pension until they reached the age of seventeen or when they had completed their schooling. In the meantime, their injury-related medical expenses were paid by the Relief Commission. Immediately following the Explosion, the commission provided financial assistance to the Halifax School for the Blind to operate free eye clinics for those who had suffered eye injuries. For decades the commission also provided an annual grant to the Canadian National Institute for the Blind for training and rehabilitation programs for blinded Explosion survivors who were registered with the CNIB.

By 1920, approximately one thousand survivors were receiving monthly pensions, and over the next fifteen years more pensioners were added as the injured children reached seventeen. By 1940, the number of pensioners

PHONE 4-1228

**THE HALIFAX RELIEF COMMISSION**
139 YOUNG STREET
HALIFAX, NOVA SCOTIA

July 17, 1957.

TO WHOM IT MAY CONCERN.

This is to certify that Eric Davidson according to the records of the Halifax Relief Commission was at the time of the Halifax Explosion (December 6, 1917) 2 years and 210 days old.

Further, our records clearly indicate that he was born on May 10, 1915.

Yours truly,

Halifax Relief Commission.

E. W. CROOKS.
SECRETARY-MANAGER.

EWC/Y.

Halifax Relief Commission letter confirming Eric's age at the time of the Halifax Explosion.

began to decrease each year from deaths. Pension increases were rare though. During the Depression years of the early 1930s, there were none. Then in 1950, the Relief Commission granted an increase to monthly pensions, raising them by 87.5 percent because they had fallen so far behind the cost of living. Many still viewed the pensions as miserly because they were considerably less than military pensions for injured soldiers even though Explosion survivors' injuries were caused by a wartime event.

My father received his first pension cheque in 1932—fifty dollars a
month for the loss of his vision. His pension remained at fifty dollars for
the next ten years. In 1942, his pension was raised to fifty-five dollars. In
1967, thirty-five years after his first cheque, he was receiving two hundred
dollars per month. He continued to receive a modest cheque each month
for the remainder of his life. My father was always grateful and he sent
several letters to the Relief Commission thanking them for their generosity
whenever an increase was granted.

Letter of July 2, 1973, to Mr. Crooks at the Halifax Relief Commission:

In reference to your recent letter that told me of the recent raise in the
pension, I wish to thank you and the other members of the Halifax
Relief Commission for this addition to the pension and wish to tell you
that it will be of great assistance to me. I also want to tell you that after
making the case to MacKinnon Optical Co. on May the 9th the eyes
were sent away and duplicated and are now very good. Thanks again, Eric
Davidson.

And an excerpt from a letter of January 4, 1976, to the Halifax Relief
Commission:

I want to say a word of thanks for the recent increase in my pension. This
will be of great help to me as living expenses are going so high these days
as we all know. I am sorry to see the Halifax Relief Commission office
closing because although I did not visit often there was always someone
there to talk to when I felt like going there. Perhaps I do not like change.
Thank you again and my best wishes for you in the New Year. Eric
Davidson.

Dad's relationship with the commission was much better than his parents'
relationship had been with it in the years following the Explosion.

In 1948, the Relief Commission's mandate was reduced to administering
pension funds only. Yet in 1949, the commission undertook a ten-year
project to develop Fort Needham into a park that the public could enjoy. The

development included a playground with a wading pool, a level sports field, and a rose garden in the south corner. Total cost was $200,000. The park was a memorial to the thousands who died or were injured in the Halifax Explosion.

Some survivors were not pleased with the commission's expenditure of funds for civic development while their pensions remained frozen. They voiced their displeasure. My father had no issue with the Fort Needham park development though, as it was a memorial as well as a recreational park the community could enjoy. When the project was complete, the Halifax Relief Commission handed maintenance of Fort Needham Memorial Park over to the City of Halifax with the understanding that the City would maintain the park for public use forever. In time, the rose garden disappeared, but the playground area and the sports field were well used for decades. The J. Eric Davidson Sport Field, as it is now named, was used for league baseball games and in recent years league football games. Eric's great-granddaughters now play and ride their bicycles in the field that bears his name.

Over the years, the Relief Commission was approached by the Province of Nova Scotia, the City, and other agencies seeking funds for a variety of projects. In 1963, the City and the Halifax Library Commission asked for funds to build a new library in central Halifax, which they said would be a memorial to the Explosion. The Relief Commission refused to commit funding as it was concerned that the pension funds would not outlive the last survivor. This concern would be proven correct.

The City and the Library Commission applied political pressure and the Relief Commission acquiesced and contributed $100,000 of survivors' pension funds for the new library. While the Relief Commission wanted the library built on one of three North End lots it owned near Fort Needham, the City and the Library Commission were adamant that the library be built in central Halifax. Wrangling continued, and in the end the library was built in central Halifax, outside of the area devastated by the Explosion. Survivors, including my father, were disappointed that they were not included in any of the decision making.

The Halifax Relief Commission lasted until 1976 when legislation was passed by the Government of Nova Scotia dissolving it. Pension funds of approximately $1.5 million were transferred to the Canadian Pension Commission to assume the responsibility of administering pension payments to approximately sixty-five individuals.

The Halifax Relief Commission Pension Continuation Act (S.C. 1974-75-76, c.88; Assented to 1976-02-25) repealed the 1918 Act respecting the Halifax Relief Commission and authorized the continuation of pensions, grants, or allowances paid by the commission. Section six of the Pension Continuation Act stated that when the last pensioner died, the Governor in Council, after consultation with the Government of Nova Scotia, could authorize the transfer of the remaining balance to a provincial or municipal body in Nova Scotia to be used for the continued rehabilitation of the area of Halifax damaged by the Explosion in 1917.

When the Canadian Pension Commission assumed the administration of the funds, it assessed each pension and found that pensioners were receiving less than they should have. It also noted that the pensions did not reflect gender equity, as a female who suffered the same injury as a male received a smaller monthly pension. The commission immediately amended pensions to reflect gender equity and to adhere to the principles set for military pensions.

J. J. Clarke, deputy chairman of the Canadian Pension Commission, wrote in a memo dated December 23, 1982, to Robert Mill, executive assistant:

> The Canadian Pension Commission is determined to provide as many and as good benefits for this group of persons as it can within the limits of the funds turned over by the Halifax Relief Commission on its dissolution.

In the same memo, J. J. Clarke remarks:

> It might be pointed out that the funds turned over to the Commission are available for pension purposes only. The Commission has no authority with respect to the rebuilding of Halifax or for making other grants, such as are requested from time to time by the City of Halifax or other organizations.

On May 25, 1987, Halifax mayor Ron Wallace wrote a letter to the Canadian Pension Commission, seeking funds from the pension fund. At that time, there were forty remaining pensioners and a fund balance of $917,646.79. Major General (Ret'd) John Wolfe, chairman of the Canadian Pension Commission, wrote to Wallace on July 13, 1987, and advised that the commission would not be releasing any funds to the City until the last pensioner had died.

At the end of January 1989, there were thirty pensioners and the balance of the fund was $791,316.08. Payments averaged $362.08 per month. Canadian Pension Commission records show that by April 1, 1992, the balance had been reduced to $630,051.38.

In 1995, Veterans Affairs Canada took over the administration of the pension fund. Veterans Affairs notified pensioners that there would not be an annual cost-of-living increase due to the pension fund's impending insolvency. This would remain the case for several more years. In 1996, Veterans Affairs and the Office of the Superintendent of Financial Institutions Canada could see the inevitability of the pension fund becoming insolvent, so a solvency guarantee was procured from the federal government.

A few years later, the pension fund did become insolvent while there were still pensioners drawing a pension, but Veterans Affairs continued to pay the monthly pensions. It did not notify pensioners of the insolvency or that the solvency guarantee had been procured.

In 2001, Dad asked me to write to Veterans Affairs on his behalf to review their stance regarding cost-of-living increases. I contacted the Honourable Ron Duhamel, Minister of Veterans Affairs, asking him to reinstate the cost-of-living allowance on the survivors' pensions. My father and I were pleasantly surprised to receive Minister Duhamel's favourable response on June 12, 2001, confirming reinstatement of the cost-of-living adjustments retroactive to 1994.

In 2001, there were only eight surviving pensioners and by 2009 there were only two, one of whom was my father. The federal government continued to fund the pension until June 2010 when the last pensioner died.

In the fall of 2012, while researching at Nova Scotia Archives, I discovered that my father's Halifax Relief Commission pension file and those of several others were not stored there. Beside Dad's file number was the word "missing." Upon further investigation, I learned that only the closed files were passed to Nova Scotia Archives by the Halifax Relief Commission when it was dissolved. My father's missing file was one of approximately sixty-five active files sent to the Canadian Pension Commission in 1976. These files were in the possession of Veterans Affairs Canada, and my concern was that the files could accidentally be destroyed after a period of years in storage. Thus began my arduous three-and-a-half-year campaign to have the missing pension files transferred to the archives.

I commenced my campaign in October 2012 and after several letters to various ministers of Veterans Affairs Canada, the files were received by the archives in March 2016. Canadian privacy laws permit my children, grandchildren, and future generations to have access to my father's file in 2029, twenty years after his death in 2009.

# Commemorating the Halifax Explosion

On December 6, 1918, the first anniversary of the Halifax Explosion, the City of Halifax held a memorial service. The guest of honour was Samuel W. McCall, governor of the Commonwealth of Massachusetts. Halifax also sent a Christmas tree to Boston in gratitude for the relief Massachusetts provided following the Explosion.

Almost seventy years would elapse before an annual civic service was held to commemorate the tremendous loss of life and the suffering of survivors. Why did this happen? The common belief is that survivors wanted to forget the tragedy. They did not want to talk about the horrors of December 6, 1917. That was certainly true of my family and my husband's family.

My husband John's family suffered a tremendous loss that day. Twelve of the Elliott family perished, along with several more of their extended family. John's grandfather George Elliott and his family survived, but George lost his mother, a brother, a sister, a sister-in-law, and several nieces and nephews. George never told his children about the family's loss, and as such the next two generations knew nothing of it until John made this shocking discovery while researching his ancestry. Like so many survivors, they did not speak of the Explosion, as they simply wished the memory of it to disappear.

During this time, when the Halifax Explosion was a fading memory for most of Nova Scotia, some Halifax-area churches remembered the day—in

Copyright Canada, 1918.                                           Halifax Disaster, Dec. 6, 1917.
DUFFUS STREET — RICHMOND SCHOOL ON LEFT

This photo shows the destruction on the Explosion. Duffus Street with Richmond School on the left.

particular, the three North End churches most affected by the Explosion: St. Mark's Anglican, St. Joseph's Roman Catholic, and United Memorial. Each held a service of commemoration each December, and sometimes the three came together in an ecumenical service.

On December 6, 1967, the fiftieth anniversary of the Explosion, a civic memorial service was held at Richmond School. In March 1968, city council passed a motion to form a committee to organize an annual commemoration service. A service organized by the city clerk's office was held in December 1968 at St. Joseph's Junior High School, but a civic memorial service would not be held again for many years.

In 1971, the Lunenburg County Christmas Tree Producers Association sent Boston a Christmas tree to promote their Christmas tree exports and to thank Massachusetts for its response to the Explosion. Nova Scotia Tourism became involved and the annual gift of a spruce tree to Boston has become a popular event. The tree is cut from a Nova Scotia property and trucked to Boston Common where there is a special tree-lighting ceremony complete with Christmas carols. I attended the Boston ceremony in 2012 with my husband and my granddaughter Ava. That year, Boston City Hall displayed an exhibit dedicated to my father, Eric Davidson.

On the sixtieth anniversary in 1977, Heritage Trust of Nova Scotia hosted a memorial evening of words and music at St. Patrick's Church in central Halifax.

Then in the early 1980s, a Scotswoman, Janet Kitz, began her archival research of the Halifax Explosion and she was shocked that there was so little local recognition in the very city where the tragedy occurred. There wasn't a monument and there wasn't a memorial service on the anniversary, unlike most cities around the world where such disasters were commemorated.

Janet's research began by documenting unclaimed personal effects of Explosion victims. These effects had been stored in boxes in the basement of Province House since 1917–1918. Janet's research resulted in her first Explosion book, *Shattered City*.

During her research, Janet sought out survivors and documented their stories. Up to this point, very few survivor stories were known locally. Janet endeared herself to survivors who trusted her with their intimate first-hand accounts of December 6, 1917. These survivors were children at the time of the Halifax Explosion and they were more eager to talk than their parents had been. Through them, Janet brought the human element forward and finally put a face to the tragedy. Her second book about the Explosion, *Survivors: Children of the Halifax Explosion,* is a compilation of these stories.

Janet was instrumental in the mounting of the original and current Halifax Explosion exhibit *Halifax Wrecked* at the Maritime Museum of the Atlantic. Her pioneering work has created public awareness. My father and Janet became very good friends, as was the case with other survivors who shared their stories with her. For many years, she held a garden party for them at her home and they looked forward to these gatherings as an opportunity to get together and reminisce outside of the solemnity of a memorial service.

In 1983, the Halifax Explosion Memorial Bells Committee was formed, spearheaded by the late Edmund Morris, former mayor of Halifax and Halifax Needham MLA. Appropriately, Janet Kitz was one of the members.

Fort Needham Memorial Park was chosen for the location of the Memorial Bell Tower because the park itself is a memorial to the victims. The tower would be built overlooking the area devastated by the Explosion with a view right down to the harbour where the tragedy happened. The committee set about raising private funds for the construction of the bell tower, and Mom and Dad were among those who donated.

On June 1, 1984, the first sod was turned on Fort Needham and on June 9, 1985, the dedication ceremony was held. Dad, Marjorie, and many survivors and their families attended. Halifax Explosion victims and survivors now had a permanent monument within the area that had been devastated, ensuring that they would not be forgotten.

Ten of the bells housed in the tower were originally donated to United Memorial Church on Kaye Street in 1920 by Barbara Orr, who lost her parents and her five siblings to the Explosion. In 1975, when the church's bell tower was deemed structurally unsafe, the bells were placed outside under a tarpaulin in front of the church. They lay there for ten years before they were installed in the newly constructed Memorial Bell Tower, along with four additional bells to complete the carillon. My wedding photos in 1975 show the bells covered by tarpaulins and resting on the lawn in front of the church.

Finally on December 6, 1985, on the occasion of the sixty-eighth anniversary, a service was held at the newly erected tower and a time capsule was placed in the tower niche. Dad attended with Marjorie and he attended every service on Fort Needham thereafter, until 2005 when his health made it impossible. For many years, Janet Kitz was the key speaker, and the same group of survivors faithfully attended each December. Survivors like Dad, Marjorie, Mary Murphy, Annie Welsh, Gordon Collins, and Edith Hartnett to name a few. There has been an annual service at the bell tower each year since.

My children and grandchildren attend with me each year. Many of the others who regularly attend have a family connection to the Explosion. The service is only held at an off-site location if the weather is too inclement, and that has rarely happened since 1985. A prayer is offered by the priest or minister from one of the churches rebuilt after the Explosion and a reception was usually held at one of these churches. United Memorial closed in 2015 and was sold to a developer. The church building was designed by renowned Halifax architect Andrew Cobb and the sanctuary is a magnificent piece of architecture. It is unfortunate that such a historic building with so strong a connection to the Halifax Explosion may be destroyed. Dad was aware that United Memorial was struggling and he bequeathed a gift from his estate, but despite the best efforts of the congregation, sadly the church could not be saved. Currently, St. Mark's Anglican is the only one of the three Explosion churches operating. St. Joseph's closed in 2006 and was demolished. An apartment complex now sits on the site.

In 2014, modernization of the Irving Shipyard saw the construction of the massive shipbuilding shed, which blocked the harbour view from the bell tower. This took everyone by surprise. There had been announcements that Irving was expanding but the public—residents of North End Halifax— were not prepared for the size of the building. When the bell tower was built in 1985, a site view was purposely designed through the trees to the harbour below.

Good news followed soon after in 2014 when Halifax regional council approved the development of a Municipal Commemorative Program to recognize the one-hundredth anniversary. A key element was the Legacy Project on Fort Needham Memorial Park. The grounds around the Halifax Explosion monument have now been improved, and a memorial plaza, with patio stones and seating, added for quiet reflection and to create a better setting for the annual service. The bells have been refurbished and the Westminster chime is rung on the hour from ten o'clock in the morning to six o'clock in the evening. The sightline from the monument to the harbour that was obstructed by the Irving building has been enhanced.

The J. Eric Davidson Sport Field was shifted south and the playground improved. Many interpretive elements have been incorporated, such as the Community Lost Railing, which runs alongside the newly constructed stairs from Union Street up to the monument. Each baluster represents a business or institution lost in the Explosion. The four Richmond churches, the schools, and several businesses are identified. The iron interpretive walls on each side of the main path to the monument have been constructed to reveal the size and manifest of the *Imo* and the *Mont Blanc*. Fort Needham,

The one-hundredth-anniversary service was held in inclement weather.

our hidden North End gem, has been given a remarkable transformation and Halifax has a magnificent memorial park to honour Explosion victims and survivors.

Also in 2014, the City called for volunteers for the Halifax Explosion 100th Anniversary Advisory Committee. I applied and was selected. The committee developed a set of guiding principles for how the centenary of the Halifax Explosion should be commemorated. It also put together a new time capsule to replace the original 1985 one.

The new time capsule will remain in the monument niche until December 6, 2067. Some of the contents are letters from Prime Minister Justin Trudeau, Queen Elizabeth II, Premier Stephen McNeil, and Mayor Mike Savage, a copy of Janet Kitz's book *Shattered City* and Paul Erikson's *History of Fort Needham*, an updated list of Explosion fatalities, newspaper articles about the one-hundredth commemoration, Canada Post's Halifax Explosion commemorative stamp, a copy of a poem by George Elliott Clarke, a one-

Parliamentary Poet Laureate George Elliott Clarke delivered a powerful and moving reading in the rain. Premier Stephen McNeil is on the left and Mayor Mike Savage is on the right of the photo.

hundredth-anniversary event program, plans for the Fort Needham Legacy project, and more.

I attended the one-hundredth-anniversary service on Fort Needham, as I do every year with my family and my brother Andrew. The weather was challenging with blustery winds and heavy rain but that did not deter the several hundred who attended. There was a canopy of umbrellas and people stood, getting blown about and pelted by rain for over an hour, but our discomfort was minor compared to what happened one hundred years earlier at this exact location and time.

At the beginning of the service, a Historic Sites and Monuments Board of Canada plaque, which will be permanently installed, was unveiled to commemorate the national significance of the Halifax Explosion.

Parliamentary Poet Laureate George Elliott Clarke powerfully recited excerpts from *Achieving Disaster, Dreaming Resurrection,* his commissioned work for the centenary. Vincent Coleman's grandson Jim Coleman spoke

Wreaths were laid during the memorial.

briefly as well. The Stadacona Band of the Royal Canadian Navy played several period pieces as well as the national anthem and "God Save the Queen."

Only one survivor, Cecelia Coolen, who was only a few days old on December 6, 1917, attended, and she received a hearty round of applause.

Descendants of Explosion victims and survivors travelled from as far away as Vancouver, California, and Scotland. Local police and firefighters were joined by Boston firefighters. At 9:04 A.M., the Citadel canon fired. Then naval and merchant ships' sirens peeled and ferry horns and church bells rang steady for one minute. It was moving. My granddaughters Isla and Mary laid a wreath in memory of the Davidson and Elliott families.

The reception after the service was held at St. Joseph's Alexander MacKay School on nearby Kaye Street where the students displayed commemorative tiles they created for the anniversary. The tiles are amazing pieces of artwork.

Marjorie (three) and Eric (one), autumn 1916.

The Halifax Regional Fire and Emergency memorial service took place at Station 4 on Lady Hammond Road. The Dartmouth Historical Society held its annual service at the *Mont Blanc* Canon Park on Albro Lake Road where a large piece of the *Mont Blanc* canon landed. In the afternoon, Halifax City Hall exhibited the contents of the 1985 and 2017 time capsules as well as other Explosion artifacts. The Halifax Central Library held an evening performance by the Nova Scotia Symphony Orchestra and George Elliott Clarke.

Commemorative events were undertaken throughout 2017. There are far too many to list but a few worth noting are the Stadacona Band's presentation of *A Moment In Time*, a musical production to commemorate the anniversary. Dalhousie Symphony Orchestra also presented a musical commemoration. *Lullaby: Inside the Halifax Explosion* is a theatre performance, which follows three diverse characters in the aftermath of the Explosion. Blair Beed and St. Patrick's Church hosted an exhibit, *People in the Face of Disaster: Remembering the Halifax Explosion*, featuring survivor stories and artifacts.

The Royal Canadian Mint issued a 14-karat gold coin but did not strike a commemorative coin for regular circulation. A limited number of gold coins were struck at a cost of almost seven hundred dollars each. The City of Halifax struck a limited number of commemorative challenge coins, and several books were launched about the Explosion.

*The Halifax Explosion* documentary was produced by Ocean Entertainment Limited for AMI (Accessible Media Inc.) and CBC television channels. It focuses on how the Explosion changed the lives of blinded survivors and how it was a catalyst for advances in the treatment of eye injuries and the formation of the CNIB. It features first-hand accounts from survivors and family members, and historians speak to the long-lasting impact of the Explosion. In the film, I speak about my father's and my grandmother's lives.

After years of near-silence, Halifax and the people of Halifax did a wonderful job of commemorating the centenary of this horrific disaster in our harbour.

# Epilogue

There was a lot of happiness in my father's world and he often said, "It's been a wonderful life."

When I was a young girl, I wished that medical science would someday make it possible for my father to see Mom, my brothers, and me, and all the world around him. Sometimes I wonder if Dad's eyes could have been saved and I wonder if decisions were made too quickly to remove his eyes. I will never know but I choose to believe that on December 6, 1917, Dr. Doull would not have removed a little boy's eyes if he had any hope that the eyes could have been mended.

Dad was a man of strong faith. He got on his knees beside the bed and prayed each night before going to sleep. He made no secret of the fact that he was grateful for his life's blessings. Many times I heard him say, "We were the lucky ones," when he spoke of surviving the Halifax Explosion.

When Dad passed away, his dear friend Reg Rasley described Dad as a "champion of courage." What a fitting description. It took courage to face the challenges of sightlessness in a sighted world. As a child, he left the security of his mother and father to attend the School for the Blind. As a young man, he bravely ventured out onto the streets of Halifax by himself with only his white cane to guide him. It took courage to become an auto mechanic when the opportunity to attend trade school was denied to him and it took courage to apply for jobs knowing that some employers would not hire a man without sight. It took courage to marry and to raise and support a family. My father was indeed a champion of courage, a real-life Superman meeting obstacles head-on.

Yet for all of Dad's tenacity, he was a humble and modest man quite happy to be just one of the boys. He seemed oblivious to the fact that many people considered him an extraordinary survivor of the Halifax Explosion.

Dad was non-judgmental and he felt deep compassion for anyone who was less fortunate than him. He believed that life was a gift and he paid it forward. He was benevolent to charities and anyone who needed a hand up whether it was family, friends, or panhandlers. He touched so many lives.

Whenever I have the opportunity to speak with people who knew my father, the recurring theme I hear from them is that Dad was a kind, compassionate, and gentle man who had the most wonderful sense of humour. Indeed he was a cheery man, never gloomy or morose, and his positive outlook on life captivated and inspired people and they were drawn to him like moths to a flame. He appreciated the things in life that people too often take for granted such as family, friendships, the peace and tranquility that nature offers, and the pure joy of living each day to the fullest.

Edith Clattenburg, née Orr, whose family suffered a tremendous loss of life in the Halifax Explosion, walked around the Halifax Commons with Dad during one of the Terry Fox runs and she said that after walking with him for a few minutes it was easy to forget that he was blind especially when he said, "See you later," as they parted ways.

To me, Dad was like any other father. After all, he could do just about anything other fathers did. But more than that he was the kindest, most loving and patient father with me and my brothers. He tucked us in each night when we were children and he taught us many life lessons as we were growing up. He urged us to never give up on our dreams and he showed us each day that anything was possible if you were determined to work for it. Indeed he was one in a million.

My father, Eric Davidson, champion of courage.

*Though it is hard to put in words*
*What my father meant to me*
*I will share with you some times with Dad*
*I hold dear in memory*

*Countless times when I was sick*
*Dad rubbed my back all night*
*And changed my laborious breathing*
*To effortless and light*

*My father and I took many trips*
*That we could laugh about all night*
*Like when we came home from Calgary*
*And only I got on the flight*

*Three days later Dad arrived home by train*
*With a smile and beard upon his face*
*For the last minute rush at the airport*
*Left Dad with the dirty clothes suitcase*

*As we shared the wonders of this world*
*Dad would ask what did I see*
*And for every vision I shared with him*
*There was something he shared with me*

*To smell the beauty of the apple blossom*
*To enjoy the morning sun upon my face*
*To hear the snaps and cracks of the wheels*
*Of a chuck wagon in a race*

*Lord in this world my Dad was not alone*
*You and my mother were always by his side*
*And I know he waits for her at heaven's gate*
*So into your kingdom together they can stride*

*Now that we celebrate my father's life*
*And all our memories make us glad*
*Let me thank you for the honour Lord*
*Of making him my Dad.*

—Andrew Davidson, son

# Acknowledgements

Writing this book has been a wonderful experience for me. I have enjoyed speaking with people who knew my father on a different level than I did. People have shared recollections about my father that were both heartwarming and humorous.

There are those who assisted me with research, editing, and so on. And some people just offered moral support. As such there are many people I must acknowledge for their various contributions to this book.

I was absolutely thrilled when Janet Kitz so kindly agreed to write the Foreword for this book. Janet has been an inspiration to me and I admire her not only for her years of research on the Halifax Explosion but also for her devotion to the survivors of the Halifax Explosion.

My thanks to Robert Huskins for sharing with me his antique automobile stories of adventures with my father. Bob is just one of the many friends Dad had who were only too happy to chauffeur and accompany Dad whenever and wherever. Thank you to Patrick Noddin, Dad's co-worker, supervisor, and dear friend for so many years. Your memories of times shared with Dad are heartwarming. To Lot Cossar, for your stories of Dad's everyday automobile advice. Your experiences with my father are an example of how Dad helped so many people remedy their car problems simply by listening to their car engines or going along for a ride with them.

To Mike Mahoney, thank you for sharing with me that Dad was an inspiration to you when you were growing up and that is why you chose him as the subject of your first film project. Thank you to Liz Rigney for sharing with me her reflections on meeting and interviewing my father.

Thank you to Blair MacKinnon and Kathy Bennett at Heritage House Law Firm for assisting my research of early Halifax real estate records pertinent to my grandparents. Of course, thanks goes to the staff at Nova Scotia Archives as well.

Special thanks to author and friend Barry Cahill for his editing assistance with the Halifax Relief Commission chapter. Thank you to authors Anne Emery and Janet Maybee who both assured me that I could write a book. To Garth Scott, Edith Clattenburg, Shirley Trites, and so many others, thank you for sharing with me your memories of my father. And special thanks to my editor, Elaine McCluskey, and to Nimbus Publishing for championing this project.

To my brothers, John and Andrew, for sharing with me some of their fondest memories of times together with our father. We shared much laughter as we journeyed together down memory lane reminiscing about all of our special memories of our father. To my daughter, Andrea, who so eloquently shared her close relationship to my parents and how that relationship inspired her choice of career. To my son, Matthew, who read my first draft and gave me helpful direction and encouragement to carry on.

Finally, I would be remiss if I did not acknowledge my grandparents, John and Georgina, and my aunts and uncles, Marjorie, June, Walter, and Jim, for the love and support they gave my father in reading automobile manuals to him and encouraging him to dream big.

# Bibliography

**Works Cited**

Bardsley, Alice. "Light in an Endless Night." *Family Herald*, Nov. 6, 1958.
Board of Managers and Superintendent, H. S. *Fifty-Eighth Annual Report*. Halifax: Halifax School for the Blind, 1928.
Kelly, G. "Public Becoming more Aware of and Helpful to Blind People." *Halifax Chronicle Herald*, p. 1, Jan. 31, 1984.
Kitz, J. F. *Shattered City: The Halifax Explosion and the Road to Recovery*. Halifax: Nimbus, 1989.
Metson, G. *The Halifax Explosion: December 6, 1917*. Toronto: McGraw Hill Ryerson, 1978.
National Film Board. *Just One of the Boys*. 1975.
Shea, H. "He's Not Just Any Mechanic." *The Atlantic Advocate*, March 1988.
Wilson, M. R. Halifax Relief Commission. Social Service Report. Halifax, 1918.

**Reference List**

Print Sources
Drew, Dick. "The Canadian Achievers." Drew Marketing & Productions, 1991.
Dalrymple, John. "Eric Davidson, Doing Things the Hard Way." *Ottawa Journal*, 1950.
Mellor, Clare. "He Never Lost Sight of Important Things." *Halifax Chronicle Herald*, Sept. 10, 2009.
Nickerson, Colin. "A World Shaken." *Globe and Mail*, December 1997.
Pugsley Fraser, Amy. "Memorial Bells Gain Renewed Appeal." *Halifax Chronicle*

*Herald,* Dec. 7, 2000.

Saunders, Doris. "Blinded Victim of Explosion Enjoys Active Life and Career."
    *Halifax Chronicle Herald,* November 1977.

*Globe and Mail.* "Blinded in the Halifax Explosion at 2, He Went on to Have a Life
    Well Lived," Sept. 11, 2009.

Ware, Beverly. "Blind Faith." *Halifax Chronicle Herald and Mail Star,* Dec. 6, 2003.


Radio and Television Sources

A&E *Sea Tales,* 1992.

*Good Morning America.* "The Halifax Explosion Story," 1996.

www.cbc.ca/archives/entry/halifax-explosion-surviving-the-disaster.

CBC Interview, J. Frank Willis, 1957.

CTV Halifax, Bill Jessome.

CTV Halifax, Liz Rigney, February 2008.

History Channel. "Growing Up Canadian."

Nova Scotia Archives.

**Photo Credits**
Photos provided by the Davidson family with the exception of:
Nova Scotia Archives: p. 18, 19, 20, 23, 34, 53, 70, 174, 182.

Milton Keynes UK
Ingram Content Group UK Ltd.
UKHW010625181124
2912UKWH00032B/177